activate your
ABUNDANCE

*Remembering Your Power To
Create What You Want*

(Also Available)

AUDIO CD

P Together Publishing

P Together Publishing

A Division of Together Publishing
www.togetherpublishing.com

This publication is designed to provide competent and reliable information regarding the subject matter covered. However, it is sold with the understanding that the author and publisher are not engaged in rendering medical and healthcare advice. Laws and practices often vary from state to state and if legal or other expert assistance is required, the services of a professional should be sought. The authors and publishers specifically disclaim any liability that is incurred from the use or application of the contents of this book.

BOOK COVER DESIGN & FORMAT:
BY MILTON CRAFT
CONTRIBUTING EDITORS:
CJ YOUNG
AMINA MCINTRYE
JESSICA LEVESQUE
RITA JAFFE
CYNDI SMITH
CHEIRO HONLOMARR
CATHERINE HUFFMAN
GRAPHICS:
AARON BAKER
PHOTOGRAPHY:
RACHEL CALDWELL
Printed in the United States of America.

ISBN: 978-0-615-42653-2

I dedicate this book to my greatest teachers Clair and Rachel and my loving husband Jimmy.

Contents

Our program consists of evening meditations, writing our goals and blessings and reading daily lessons.

My philosophy is to have all the tools available to us so that we can use them when needed. I share tools with you here that are tried, tested and work.

INTRODUCTION

"Listen for the magic word of motivation and you will hear it. Then the sky is the limit."

---Norman Vincent Peale

Alright, so you grabbed a book about abundance - smart person! Well, the message here may be a little different than you were expecting. There are no accidents. You picked this book up now because you are becoming conscious and ready to make a shift in your abundance on all levels -- mentally, physically and spiritually. This is done by simply connecting to the part of you that is Divine. The dominant intent of this book is to remind you of how brilliant and powerful you are, and to help you take full responsibility for your life. The path to our well-being is always calling us. We will, through lifting our thoughts, consciously connect with the part of us that is Divine and holds the answers we seek. I want to be clear: You Are Perfect - we are simply building on where we are. Most of the ideas presented here will feel very familiar, like, "Oh yes, I knew that, I just needed to be reminded."

You are now at the perfect time and place in your life. When you understand this, we are in agreement. If you do not feel this way now, we intend to spend a little time together and raise our consciousness. We will focus on getting very happy with where we are. This is our ultimate goal. We will lift our minds and perspectives and then enjoy the natural evolution of many things we have always wanted coming to us with ease as if by magic. I feel blessed to know that we all have the same access to this

Introduction

Divine Connection which will enhance us on all levels. I love sharing this knowledge with others who are ready.

True abundance is about having all the vitality, love and wealth we desire. It is also about having peace of mind and loving the life we have. We spend time now to care about what a miracle we are and that the connection to our personal God is where all our power lies. You may call this God, Jesus, Buddha, your higher self or any name you are comfortable with. It is not my intention to explain the unexplainable, only to remind us to reach and connect with this Divine Power on a more regular basis. For our purposes, we will be using the term "God" and/or the word "Divine" to describe this energy.

I was fortunate to become the host of a radio show this past year. The theme of the show quickly evolved into how we can feel good emotionally, which is so important to a successful life. I was honored to interview many brilliant authors and experts on how we can feel good now. This book is the culmination of information obtained from these enlightening interviews and years of studying many people I consider to be masters at the art of feeling good now.

One of the most important messages this book offers is how negative emotions become trapped in our body, creating dis-ease and problems in our lives. Many of us have lived with these problems for years, unaware of the root cause. These include weight, relationship, health and financial problems. You are probably thinking, "If I need to lose weight, how will

 xi

Introduction

clearing negative emotions help?" Let me assure you that releasing these heavy emotions will lighten our load both mentally and physically. I have found some of the best techniques available to heal and clear these negative emotions. I present them here to you with the knowing that they will make wonderful shifts in your consciousness if practiced consistently with an open mind. The dividends for releasing these stuck negative emotions are endless. You will discover yourself in a new way as all your best qualities start to emerge. This is a result of becoming conscious and setting the intention to create a space for the Divine you to emerge.

In *Activate Your Abundance,* you will also discover a 44-day program designed to support you and focus on how blessed you are by nature. We will do the Divine meditations in this book before bed each night to lift our mind on a consistent basis. You may also find audios of these meditations that were created for your listening pleasure at www.togetherpublishing.com. As part of our program, we also intend to spend time each day reading about the blessings in our lives and writing out our fondest desires.

These activities done together on a consistent, personal basis will create joy in our mindset and set the stage for blessings to flow into every area of our life. They will also ground us firmly into our powerful *now* and knowing all is well. **All our power is in the *now*.**

If, however, this is not the right time for you to discover this 44-day program, simply enjoy the rest of the book. The message is charged to uplift our mood and attitude. You will feel

Introduction

better every time you read it, like a good friend encouraging you. We will cover an array of prosperity and vitality techniques that have been practiced with great success by abundant thinkers around the world. There is something here for everyone. You know what will work for you. **Take the best and leave the rest.**

You are a vibrating center of vitality and prosperity; *now* is the moment to start seeing yourself this way. You have as much Divine wisdom as anyone you have ever met or admired.

In this work, we recognize that we all go through seeming difficult periods in our lives; not every moment appears happy, yet every moment is perfect. This book is designed to help with life. The challenging periods in our lives need to be understood for the dynamic, creating experiences they are and how they contribute to our becoming more than we ever imagined.

I have been through some very unwanted situations in my life and I feel blessed to be at the level of consciousness where I understand that they have made me the person I am today. These challenges have made me search for the answers I share here and have given me a much closer connection to my God.

It is such a great attitude to bless challenges and understand the importance they play in our lives. The caterpillar will go through some pain in order to become a butterfly. We are all works in progress; we are never complete. There is always something to look forward to.

Introduction

We are all connected and changing the world one thought at a time. A massive collection of thoughts and feelings exists, which we call our "collective consciousness." Every thought and emotion exists here. There are parts of the collective consciousness that are filled with "lack and fear" based thoughts, and it is easy to get caught up in this. As we clean up our own thoughts, it helps us, and everyone on the planet. We are all connected. We are healing the planet as we heal ourselves. Have you heard of the "hundred monkey theory?" It goes something like this:

There are 2 groups of monkeys on islands completely separated by water that cannot see each other. On one island a monkey starts using a coconut shell to drink water from. The other monkeys start copying the leader slowly but surely. Finally 100 monkeys are drinking their water from a coconut shell. The monkeys on the other island start doing the same thing without having seen this activity.

It is the connection of like minds that sends this message and creates change. We all thrive when we immerse ourselves in positive information and practice consistently staying in a good place mentally. The dividends are endless.

A "prosperity consciousness" is where all our power lies. The saying "as above, so below" explains this. We must first feel prosperous on the inside in order for love and abundance to manifest in our life.

Introduction

When one speaks of their lack, I want to infuse them with the knowledge that we really are dynamic, intuitive creators. All we have to do is shift our thinking a little and we will be shown very quickly that this is true.

Of course, when people are going through particularly difficult periods, this might be difficult to hear, but when the student is ready, the teacher appears.

Lifting our thinking is a bit of a process and happens a little every day; this is the way to flow and feel comfortable with our transition. What is becoming quite clear to many is we have so much more creative ability than we ever knew. Our true power lies in our connection to God, love, appreciation of where we are and alignment of thought. Once a person cleans up their thinking just a little and the miracles start flowing in, it just feels natural.

Let me ask you this: Are you going to be one of the people who allows thoughts of fear and scarcity to keep you down, or do you want to *Activate Your Abundance* now and allow what you desire and deserve to flow to you? There are no coincidences. I believe if you have found this book, you are becoming conscious and lifting now.

Ultimately it is you and God who allow all that is necessary to reap the rewards. No one can do this for you, but you. When we accept this personal responsibility with love, we are on our way and in our power. So let's get started. *Activate Your Abundance* now.

THE PROGRAM

ABOUT YOUR 44-DAY PROGRAM

"Every day remind yourself of your own ability, of your good mind and affirm that you can make something really good out of your life."

---Norman Vincent Peale

Let's get started on the 44-day *Activate Your Abundance* program right away. Our program consists of evening meditations, writing our goals and blessings and reading daily lessons. The main point is to start lifting our consciousness and self-worth *now* to allow a lifted mindset. If this is not Divine timing for your program, simply enjoy the book and participate in the program when you are ready.

You may use one, a combination, or all of the ideas in this book. Timing is also important. An idea that works great today may need to be boosted or traded for another one in the future. You have the best understanding of what will work for you and when; the longer you practice, the more confident you become. The only rules are to do what feels best and enjoy the process.

These positive concepts start lifting you without any effort on your part. You might notice that you just start relaxing more often and feel better about yourself. Let all the components come together in their own time and enjoy the experience.

The Program

Take care in knowing that in the event things feel shaken up or upsetting at times, this is what the great Catherine Ponder calls "Chemicalization," or simply that sometimes things appear worse before they get better. This is just the old stale energies being released so that we can make room for the new empowering ones. This is a good thing; just accept where you are and know that everything is in Divine Order. Things will get better. Have faith!

As you begin this program, do not talk about it with anyone that is not encouraging and supportive. It is best to do this program in secrecy as long as possible. This yields much better results, as it gives this knowledge time to take root. Maybe there is someone you believe would enhance your program. By all means feel free to share, but keeping this bond between you and your God is truly the most encouraging way to begin. You know how to proceed.

Be receptive to the message of how magnificent you are. If that little voice in your head says, "This is silly," then tell it, "Thank you for sharing," and continue with your program.

Now let's create a powerful positive mindset that allows us to be the radiating center of joy, vitality and prosperity we are!

PART I - MEDITATIONS

There are 11 different nightly meditations. We shall meditate on the first one for four nights in a row and then move onto the next meditation for the next four nights. Each meditation is clearly labeled for you. We shall continue this pattern until we have completed all 11 meditations, which will take a total of 44 nights.

Read each meditation slowly, giving it time to sink in. Allow the message of how worthy you are to go deep into your heart and mind. Or go to www.togetherpublishing.com to get the meditation audios for your listening pleasure.

When we start focusing on these truths consistently, our consciousness shifts. As our mind and heart lift, this affects our whole world in a very positive way. Know that love, vitality and prosperity start with a lifted consciousness first, then manifest in our world.

KEY POINTS TO GET FROM THE MEDITATIONS

The meditations we are about to embark upon have a very uplifting message. Here are the key points to understand and focus on during and after our meditations.

1. Connection to our God-energy is the key to feeling our best and accomplishing great things. Staying conscious of this connection and in the moment is our main job.

2. We are worthy and perfect just as we are. We are God's greatest miracle. Just feel this. Feel your Divinity and cultivate deep self-love.

3. No person, account or job is the source of our abundance or well-being. **Our connection to and knowing that God is**

never ending prosperity is the source of our supply, vitality and happiness. This Divine Energy is you; thus you are your own supply. Once we use care to focus on our connection to Divine intelligence and stop looking for the money or condition to make us happy, we will be the powerful creator we came here to be. This Divine connection creates bliss and peace like nothing else can. As we practice and get this knowledge deep in our mind and heart, we will experience great peace and a content feeling, free from fear and worry.

4. Appreciation is our finest tool; practice it daily. Count your blessings, not your problems.

Anytime you are having a rough patch, pull out one of these meditations and let it fill you with love and peace.

PART 2

WRITING OUR GOALS AND BLESSINGS

"Have great hopes and dare to go all out for them. Have great dreams and dare to live them. Have tremendous expectations and believe in them."

---Norman Vincent Peale

The second part of our program consists of writing out our blessings and goals to harness the power of the written word combined with Divine mind. Each morning, we shall read over our

 4

The Program

daily section and then write our goals, blessings and desired life for 15 minutes.

This is a form of goal setting. Writing out what we love now and are going to accomplish sends a strong message to our subconscious and the universe that we shall thrive. It has been proven time and time again that when we write out goals, they come into being much easier as we unleash energies that we cannot see but feel. It is so illuminating to know that things do move in Divine Order. Things start lining up and falling into place after writing them down.

Making a list of things that need to be accomplished for the day, first thing in the morning, is a great way to get ourselves focused and going. It always amazes me how things on my list just "magically" get done.

Setting goals is so important. When some people retire, the reason they have problems is because they need goals to keep them focused and vital. We all need something to look forward to, no matter what our age.

A while back, I set a goal to make motivational audio CDs. I had absolutely no idea how to go about this but wrote it out as a goal just the same. I was later contacted and asked to be the host of a radio show. I knew nothing about radio, but I was very excited to learn that I would be trained in creating audio programs. It always amazes me how we are being led down this path; I really stand in awe.

The Program

As you write out your desired life map every morning of your program, think:

Goal Setting + Appreciation = Desired Results

This may sound a little tricky, but just start relaxing and writing it out. During the program, we will be getting up 15 minutes earlier in the morning to devote time to writing and reading about the perfect life we are experiencing and creating. We start by writing out all the things we appreciate. Get very creative and look for all your blessings. For those that say they cannot think of any blessings, listing that your beautiful eyes can see this is a wonderful start. List your strong mind, beating heart and lungs that work nonstop as just a few more of your miraculous blessings. Sit and quiet your mind to listen for all your blessings -- There are too many to count! Simply get started and practice. Your abundance meditations train you to quiet the mind and look for what you enjoy.

After you have written out your blessings, you will be in a lifted state of mind and ready to write out every aspect of your life becoming the way you want it. Set your goals. Write everything as if you already are experiencing it. Writing in present tense empowers your ideas. Write about all the beautiful relationships you are experiencing and how comfortable and serene your home is. Describe how fulfilling and prosperous your life's work is, how vibrant and attractive you are. If you do not know what you want your life's work is to be, this is fine. Simply make happy statements that leave room for Divine Energy to fill in the blanks.

The Program

For example, you might say: "I have a fulfilling prosperous career in which I get to help many. I enjoy what I do so much it feels like I am playing at a job."

This is for your eyes only, so be fearless. Dare to dream! Each day, spend at least 10 to 15 minutes writing and reading your list with pure joy; this is the second part of your program. You may add to your list when inspired and continue to let it evolve into a Divine picture. As you practice, you may have days that feel better than others. Be easy on yourself! Just keep trying - it all falls into place with patience. Have faith. Keep a journal you can build on every day.

Your first meditation for nights 1-4 is found ahead after we explore the power of imagination to enhance your daily writing of goals and blessings and a section with some valuable tools to help you clear and enhance your life. Then, you will find your other 10 evening meditations individually placed between 4 daily lessons and a bonus. Expect miracles! Refer to your table of contents for a guide.

Enjoy the next 44 days and let them be an adventurous launching pad to all the blessings that you deserve. **Mark this day on your calendar and count up at least 44 days to start your new life and new you. Each day after you complete your program, record it on the chart ahead. Shade in the top half of your box when you start the morning with your appreciation, goal setting and positive life map. Shade in the bottom half of**

The Program

the box when you complete your Divine meditation at night. Be consistent and complete your 44 days and nights for Divine results.

Start Date _____

1	2	3	4	5	6	7	8	9	10	11
12	13	14	15	16	17	18	19	20	21	22
23	24	25	26	27	28	29	30	31	32	33
34	35	36	37	38	39	40	41	42	43	44

Finish Date _____

 8

The Program

IMAGINATION, YOUR KINGDOM

"Vision is the art of seeing things invisible."

---Jonathan Swift

The more we learn about imagination, the more obvious it becomes that this is a skill we want to practice and develop.

I had an important experience as a child. I was sitting in the school gym wishing I had more friends. Out of the blue, I started seeing myself as very powerful. I saw myself like a superhero flying to the top of the high gym ceiling where everyone could see me. I felt so empowered imagining myself flying around the gym while all the kids were thinking how cool it looked. I loved how this felt and it became a recurring "fantasy" that year in school.

Soon after, I became friends with a girl who had me try out for a sports team with her. I had never experienced the intense friendships that can develop as a result of team sports. I made many wonderful new friends and life just got more fun. It was one of the best years of my childhood, I always remember fondly. One of my teachers even signed my yearbook, "Kim, I have never seen a person make such a wonderful transformation."

I now know for certain that this daydreaming of being a superhero brought me a magnificent year and many friends. For me, this consistent "fantasy" made me feel empowered, flowing over into other areas of my life. It is the activity of feeling good that starts to shift things. The creative force of the universe does

The Program

not know if these pictures in your mind are real or not; it simply responds to the feelings these pictures create. This is taught by masters like Neville and Abraham-Hicks and then tried and proven by many. Your dominant visions may vary, but your goal is to see yourself in your power, doing something you love, and feeling great.

My point is that there have been specific times in our lives where we unknowingly use imagination to get what we desire. We do not always know that we are doing this, only following an instinct. Birds are not trained to fly south for the winter; they just know. We all have these same instincts. We simply need to listen for Divine Intelligence.

Let's go over some general ideas to help you write out your desired life map during your 44-day program. Writing these "coming attractions" down should be a pleasure. Start with the intent to imagine things just as you want them. Find things to think about that bring you joy and pleasure. See yourself thriving in all the ways you have always wanted. I will give some general guidelines here, just to get you started. You can get your own fulfilling "mind movies" going that you enjoy.

Imagine yourself feeling more attractive, joyful and peaceful than ever. See yourself in the perfect outfit that makes you look fit and attractive. You are glowing with vitality, laughing and smiling from ear to ear. Now, see yourself doing something you love. If you cannot immediately think of something, borrow activities of others you admire and try them out. Keep at it until you find something that makes you feel great. The choices are endless. Just play with it; make this fun.

You may want to bring someone else you enjoy into your scene. I love to see myself laughing and playing with people I love; this creates wonderful relationships. You could even see yourself enjoying time with a famous person that you admire if that feels good. The whole key is to play with images that feel good. Imagine beautiful surroundings, beaches, homes or destinations. The sky is really the limit as you practice feeling good while relaxing; the possibilities are endless!

Practice daydreaming whenever possible! Play a game where every time you are in line at the store, you go into your imagining place and see yourself as a superhero, rock star, speaker that inspires others or any other idea that brings you into your power in a joyful way. You may want to go walking on a fabulous beach with an incredible person you admire. Get creative and, most important, enjoy.

Imagination is one of the most potent tools in your toolbox and now you can use it to create a fulfilling and happy life. This is why children are such powerful creators and can be happy in almost any circumstance. They are wonderful at imagination and go into all kinds of games that please them. This is also why certain people are so powerful and seem to just get anything they want. They are connected to Divine Imagination and are creating and enjoying as they go. They are using the full force of their imagination to get what they want, many times without even

The Program

knowing it. Imagination develops into their greatest skill. You and I can easily do this as well. As we practice seeing things the way we want them, we will feel better on a regular basis. More things we want will come to us. This is a powerful knowing and I want to inspire you to think big.

Imagination is where we level the playing field. We all have the same ability to imagine what we want. It is just a matter of enjoying the process and being conscious of our ability to create. We want to take on the childlike qualities of joy and imagination to help create the incredible life that we know from the deepest place in our soul we deserve. We deserve to feel brilliant and fulfilled. Let's get started now and set the intention to go into imagination as often as possible. What a wonderful skill to replace being bored or criticizing with magnificent fantasies that make us feel great.

Here we go: picture yourself on a stage performing for people who adore you. They are smiling and cheering as you entertain them. You are in the zone as you move with grace and ease across the stage performing your favorite music or dance routine. Listen to your favorite music that moves you while you do this. You are in your power and full of love. Add this picture to your exercise routine, fueling your vision with extra life-enhancing oxygen.

The Program

Or you could see yourself giving an inspiring workshop, encouraging people to be the best they can be. You may prefer to see yourself excelling as a professional athlete, enjoying a beautiful Hawaiian golf course. Then, go hang out with your friends after the match, while laughing and enjoying each other's company. See yourself riding a beautiful horse gracefully on the beach, the wind blowing in your hair and invigorating your skin while you enjoy a perfect sunset. See yourself walking and holding hands with someone you adore on a beautiful beach. The water is crystal blue and the sand is white on a sunny, beautiful day.

Neville Goddard was an influential new thought teacher. His books have guided many to their dreams and desires. Goddard explains that picturing what we want on an ongoing basis is the key to having the life we desire. As we make it a priority to visualize our fondest desires, we tap into a very pleasant way to spend time and encourage good moods.

In college, I had some challenges graduating. When it got to the point that I really needed to buckle down and get my diploma, an interesting thing happened. Every night I would lie in bed and get the strongest picture of myself walking down the aisle in my beautiful white cap and graduation gown to receive my diploma. I would see myself on the stage receiving my diploma and feeling so proud. Even though I had struggled and felt I was receiving little guidance, I graduated within the year. I am not even sure why I did it. I just kept getting this picture in my mind and

The Program

enjoying it. I am now positive that my graduation was helped along by Divine guidance. It was an amazing and telling experience.

As we become conscious of our imagination's ability to enhance our lives and remember to use it on a regular basis, we shall thrive. You may want to put some reminder notes in places you will see. You can put little reminders to imagine what you want on your bathroom mirror, refrigerator or desk. This way you can get in the habit of seeing your life flowing in a perfect way that pleases you. See yourself thriving and prospering in magnificent ways. You can do this anywhere, anytime. So how about now?

TOOLS FOR OUR TOOLBOX

"Luck is what happens when preparation meets opportunity."

---Seneca

My philosophy is to have all the tools available to us so that we can use them when needed. I share tools with you here that are tried, tested and work. These tools are most effective when you apply and practice the ones you resonate with. Many of these come from people considered to be masters at the art of feeling good and lining up with what they want. We will explore the work of "Divine teachers" such as John Randolf Price, Og Mandino, Abraham-Hicks, Catherine Ponder, Florence Shinn, Deepak Chopra and James Mangan. We take their teachings and combine them with years of experience to give you many options to choose from.

We are living in unprecedented times where technology and ideas are being shared at the speed of light with the Internet. This gives us all of the best teachings available today from the past and present. They come together here and create a wonderful alchemy, being blended together today in a way that has never been possible. This gives us all access to wake up and connect with our God selves stronger than ever. It is truly the time of awakening. Anyone who is seeking this information will find it. It is becoming more and more accepted that we co-create our own reality and now is the perfect time to learn more and practice.

Tools for Our Toolbox

AN INVALUABLE TOOL: EMOTIONAL FREEDOM TECHNIQUE (EFT)

"Most of our emotional and physical problems are caused (or contributed to) by our unresolved specific events, the vast majority of which can be easily handled by EFT."

---Gary Craig

The most important skill we can develop is the ability to identify and release unwelcome thoughts and emotions from our mind and body. Once we understand that our thoughts and beliefs are creating our reality, it is common to become afraid of our negative thoughts. EFT, also known as tapping, is the perfect enhancement to any program that encourages positive thought because it creates vast spaces in the mind for new uplifting thought to enter. EFT is a simple and effective tool discovered by Gary Craig that releases unwanted thoughts and emotions in order to reclaim untold peace. The priceless information presented here is also inspired by Natalie Hill, an experienced EFT practitioner.

EFT works with specific energy meridians we have throughout our body. We may tap on these points while holding an unpleasant thought with the **intention** of releasing this negative thought. Dr. Bradley Nelson, author of *The Emotion Code*, states, **"Intention is a powerful form of thought-energy. It is possible to release trapped emotions using the power of your intention alone. I believe that the intention to release the trapped emotion is really the most important part of the equation."**

16

Tools for Our Toolbox

The negative programs, thoughts and beliefs we hold actually start to drain our energy and create physical problems. Most people carry around these negative emotions for years without being aware that they are contributing to many of the problems and diseases they are experiencing today. It is to our benefit to clear out these self-defeating thoughts, much like clearing the clutter from our home. When we practice tapping we will start to feel lighter and happier. As a result, Divine ideas will start to come and delight us.

The intelligent practice of tapping is related to the science of acupuncture that dates back 2500 years. When we become conscious that we are holding a thought that feels uncomfortable, we can start tapping on the energy points and get relief. It feels like the tension just releases and we can think clearly again. For me it feels like an actual sigh of relief. The anger, depression, fear or even unwanted physical symptoms will simply become less prevalent. Be patient and keep at it. We may even find ourselves laughing as these thoughts lift and we feel relief.

Here is how to tap away your negative emotions and thoughts. Always use the tips of your fingers as they have their own energy meridians. This gives us double benefits. We may tap with our left or right hand; choose the one most comfortable, knowing you may switch hands when needed.

We want to clear on negative beliefs that keep popping up like, "I never have enough money," "I am not good enough," or "I need to lose weight." Of course you have your own personal negative beliefs you want to clear. Understand this: the act of clearing out these self-defeating beliefs is one of the most empowering practices we can do. Without these negative thoughts running rampant in our minds, we will start attracting the life we truly desire.

We may also tap on physical pains such as a stomachache or headache. There is a connection between the stomachache (and any unwanted condition) and the worrying. We start by tapping on our karate chop point (shown picture 1) and saying, "Even though I have this headache, I still love and accept myself." Now, listen for any thoughts that come up like, "Wow, this job feels like too much for one person to handle," and tap on that. We simply want to listen for what comes up and tap on it. The great thing about tapping is we are allowed to complain and vent out these negative emotions with the intention of clearing them out for good and feeling better. Our complaining actually serves a purpose when combined with tapping.

Let's do a round of tapping here. Let's tap on the common issue of feeling anxious. Of course, you may substitute any fear or negative thought you are dealing with and want to clear. Try this:

Tools for Our Toolbox

Picture 1   Karate Chop Point

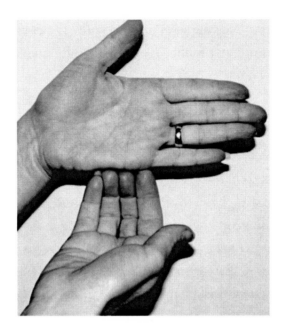

Picture taken by Rachel Caldwell

1. Start by tapping on the side of your hand (see Figure 1) and say the setup statement, "Even though I feel anxious, I still love and accept myself." Say this set up statement 3 times. Keep tapping on your hand as you say your setup statement.

2. Now, move to your face meridians (all face meridians are shown on Figure 2). On the rest of these points we will just say a reminder phrase once

and move to the next point. The reminder phrase keeps you focused on the issue so tapping on these points can get the energy moving and allow healing and change. The first meridian we tap on is the eyebrow point. Tap on this area while saying, "This anxious feeling." **The more you can feel the negative emotion while tapping the more effective the release will be.** When you go into the deep negative feeling of the stress while tapping, this is helping to release it for good.

3. Now, move to the side of your eye and tap. As you tap on this spot, continue to say the negative thought or condition, "This anxiety is making me cranky." Be open to any thoughts that come up and tap on them. For example, if the feeling, "I am tired of people criticizing me," comes up, tap while you say it.

4. Now tap on the spot under the eye and say, "This nervousness feels like it will never go away."

5. Now tap on the spot under the nose and continue to vent, "This anxiety scares me and makes me feel helpless."

6. Now tap on the chin where the diagram shows and say, "This feeling like I will never get everything done, this nervousness in my body."

Tools for Our Toolbox

7. Now tap on your collarbone while making another statement that comes up like, "I hate feeling so anxious."

8. Now tap all over the top of your head with the tip of all your fingers and make another statement, "I am tired of this tension in my body that feels like it will never go away."

You have completed one round of tapping; it should go relatively quickly. Take a deep breath and just sit with yourself for a minute. Now it is time to evaluate. How do you feel? Has the unwanted emotion or feeling calmed down? If not, you may do another round of tapping until you feel the relief.

Once you feel relief, it is time to do a round of, "Wouldn't it be nice if...?" Be sure you feel ready before you start this round. If the tapping has not given you relief yet, continue to tap on the problem or take a break. If we try to move to our "Wouldn't it be nice if...?" round before we are ready, the mind will create arguments. When we do our "Wouldn't it be nice if...?" round, it should feel good like, "Yes, everything is feeling a lot better now." Take your time. Tapping may feel foreign to you at first.

In this round we put the question, "Wouldn't it be nice if...?" in front of desired statements. This allows our minds to accept these statements easier. Start tapping on your energy points shown below and make statements like, "Wouldn't it be nice if I could relax more often?" or "Wouldn't it be nice if I could go with the flow and enjoy my days more?" or "Wouldn't it be nice if I remembered my ability to attract the perfect people to help me?" Keep tapping on your energy meridians while you make these statements.

Once you feel good making your "Wouldn't it be nice if…?" statements, it is time to move right into your definite statements about what you do want with joy and knowing, like positive affirmations. Here are a few examples: "Everything is going to be alright," "I am managing my time better every day," and "I am going to get all the help I need." Now, we are commanding and back in our power.

Figure 2: Created by Aaron Baker of 501 graphicdesign.com

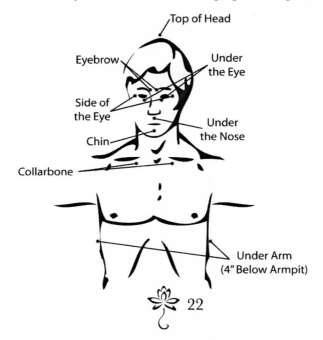

Tools for Our Toolbox

Tapping is like anything else -- the more we do it, the better we will understand how we are responding and how much we need to practice. We get better the longer we practice. If you are having trouble believing that something so silly and simple could work, you will want to tap on that. For example, while tapping say, "Even though this is silly and will never work, I still love and accept myself."

If you find yourself in public experiencing negative emotion, there is a discreet way to tap. Natalie Hill explains that right when we feel the stressful emotion is the time to tap it out. If we are somewhere it is inappropriate to tap on our face, we may use the finger tapping technique just as effectively instead. Simply tap the right side of the nail on your pointer finger with your thumb. Tap your thumb and finger together about 10 times while saying the negative thought to yourself that is bothering you. Then, tap the side of each other finger with your thumb, just like you did your pointer finger. This way you may clear negative emotions anywhere, anytime.

Natalie Hill suggests that we make a written list of anything that has ever bothered us. Try to come up with as many as possible; at least 100 are a good start. Each day, tap on three of these issues. This cultivates a feeling of peace in our lives. Give this tapping technique a try and expect miracles.

Tools for Our Toolbox

ANCIENT HAWAIIAN SECRET

"To be wronged is nothing unless you continue to remember it."

---Confucius

When we experience negative thoughts about someone, we are in that moment holding ourselves away from everything we want. If we happen to desire to be free of this person, we are actually creating an energetic link that is stronger than steel. We are all going to have these thoughts from time to time as we are human, but whether we entertain them or not is up to us. It is in our best interest to clean them up. Do not be hard on yourself for these unwanted thoughts; simply make the decision to stay conscious and lift yourself as often as possible.

Ho'oponopono has been practiced by Hawaiian masters for centuries. Ho'oponopono is the art of sending forgiveness and love to any unwanted situation or person around you. **This begins with the powerful understanding that peace begins with me.** Understanding that everything in our life is a reflection of what is going on in our heart and mind. Once we realize this, we are in our power. **We do not have to look to one other person to change or do something different in order to thrive. We may take full responsibility for any situation in our lives and clean it up. This is where our true power lies.**

Tools for Our Toolbox

The process is very simple. When we think about an unwanted situation or person, we say to ourselves "I love you," "I am sorry," "Please forgive me," "I forgive you," "Thank you." This immediately starts cleaning and clearing negative memories and emotions from us. This in turn will clear out old conscious and subconscious programs, creating a new space for wonderful new thoughts and blessings to come.

You may be asking, "Why should I take responsibility, when it is the other person's fault?" **This is where we separate the victims from the powerful creators.** Once we start taking full responsibility and realize our true power to clean up everything in our life, we are on our way to true peace of mind and blessings. **When we think negative thoughts about another person or situation, the reason it feels so bad is because this is a departure from whom we truly are and where our power lies. We really feel our best when we are sending love and thinking thoughts that uplift us and others. When we uplift another, we uplift ourselves.** It really is that simple.

As we clear years of old accumulated negative thoughts with Ho'oponopono or any other powerful techniques, we are opening up our mind to pure brilliance. We start to be on the receiving end of magnificent ideas. Empowering ideas we never even considered concerning well-being, relationships and income will flow to us. It is not us having these ideas, but the Divine Mind flowing through the clear channel we have created with Love. We can see things in a whole new way when we release resentments

Tools for Our Toolbox

blocking our well-being and abundance. The windows become clear and we can see things in a fresh new light. It will become so obvious what a Divine being we are when we pair with God and clear our channel.

This is our birthright. Would you allow some negative thoughts about another to keep you from it? This is big: release these negative self-destructive thoughts and experience more of the abundance and happiness we deserve. It is a constant process, as we are all human and going to have negative judgments. We can, however, lift our minds on a consistent basis, get conscious and reap the never-ending dividends.

Another wonderful technique we can use is to "turn light" on a person. For example, let's say we are having problems with a good friend, family member or even a "perceived enemy," we can simply say:

*Light switch on me (*say your name*), and light switch on them* (say their name*)*.

So, for example if I am having "perceived" problems with Sally, I would say, "Light switch on Kim, light switch on Sally." Have faith because it is working miracles on subtle levels. Every time you think the negative thoughts, say it again, "Light switch on me, light switch on them." Always say your name first remembering that you are protected and guided.

Tools for Our Toolbox

Do this for yourself. As we release resentment and negative feelings, we will feel better and set a shining example for those around us. We will no longer be part of a "herd" mentality that says, "It is the other guy's fault." Does it ever do any good to blame others? We are becoming far too smart to continue to blame others and expect things to change. Align your mind-set with the knowledge that when you forgive and love others, you are consciously lifting yourself to the beautiful place you deserve to be. "I love you," "I am sorry," "Please forgive me," "I forgive you" and "Thank you" are words to live by. We are on your way to true peace and blessings.

SPEAK SUCCESSFULLY

"Remind yourself that loving words and loving thoughts seem supercharged with power to produce good."

---Catherine Ponder

When I occasionally overhear someone complaining about his or her perceived lack of abundance, I understand that they are coming from a place of fear. That is the great gift John Randolph Price, Catherine Ponder, Florence Shinn, Deepak Chopra, Wayne Dyer and many other teachers have given us. They have reminded us that a strong connection to Divine wisdom will lead us to the things we desire, **if they are for our highest good.**

When I encounter people caught up in a scarcity and fear mentality, I want to instill their power back to them. Of course, each person must do this for himself or herself. I want to explain that speaking about what we want really serves us well. We do not want lack, so we want to stop speaking of it.

The poignant book *Your Word Is Your Wand* by Florence Shinn says it all. Your words are creating, so pay attention and use them to your advantage.

James Mangan gave us *The Secret Of Perfect Living* in the 1960s. Mangan explains that there are certain words that can be used with intention to get more of what we want. He coined the phrase "Switchwords." These power words will turn on our subconscious like a switch to help us get more of what we want. Mangan spent most of his life researching and finding these words for us. For those of us who connect with them, they are a wonderful tool for creating and enjoying life more.

These words have been known to help people with all kinds of situations. I have a dear friend who called me upset because she was overseas in Paris, France and lost her purse. She was in a little shop and set it down. She walked away and soon realized it was gone. By the time she went back to find her purse, no one knew where it was. She called me crying and worried that she would be without funds for the rest of her trip. I told her to remain calm and say the Switchword "Reach" anytime she worried about her purse. Her credit card was canceled and she was sent funds to enjoy the remainder of her trip. Anytime she thought about her purse she said, "Reach". She told me that she must have said "Reach" a thousand times.

Tools for Our Toolbox

The next day the Paris police called her. They had her purse and wanted to make arrangements to return it. She called me ecstatic with the wonderful news. Her purse was returned with all her money and credit card in it. This is just one of many miracles created with Switchwords. Needless to say, "Reach" is one of my favorite Switchwords and I use it with success to find anything lost.

I will share some of the words that allow more prosperity of health, love and wealth *now*:

FIND - "to find a fortune." Say, "Find," when you want to attract wealth and abundance.

BE - to be in radiant health and connected to our God mind.

COUNT - to attract money. The theory behind this word is that every time we see a pile of coins lying around, we automatically start counting them in our mind.

DIVINE - to create the extraordinary (or miracle). I get wonderful results with the word Divine and use it in all my combinations, which we will discuss next.

TOGETHER - is the master Switchword. Together pulls together our conscious, subconscious and super-conscious to bring out the best in us -- to bring out our God Self.

Tools for Our Toolbox

LOVE - Love is, of course, the most powerful force in the world. When we say "Love," it wraps a healing energy around the person who sends it and the receiver.

WHOLE - to understand that we have everything we need within ourselves. There is no need to look for it in another.

PLETHORA - I discovered the word "Plethora" during a period when I wanted to constantly remind myself that there is more than enough of everything for everyone. Competition for resources is an illusion. There is a plethora of health, money and mates.

REACH - "Reach" is one of my favorite Switchwords. We can use reach to find anything we have lost. Simply say reach and go about your business. You will be guided to what you are looking for in the perfect time. Reach can also be used to reach emotional states like joy and bliss.

We will also benefit by using combinations of the Switchwords. Here are some suggestions:

TOGETHER DIVINE LOVE - this activates love in any relationship or situation. It is perfect for solving fights and communication problems. This combination will create wonderful results when said to yourself or aloud with intention.

TOGETHER DIVINE FIND COUNT - this combination creates wealth and income when said consistently with belief.

Tools for Our Toolbox

BE TOGETHER DIVINE - this combination may be used to attract vibrant health on all levels.

DIVINE TIMING - if you ever find yourself needing things to move faster than they are, simply say, "Divine timing," and remind yourself that everything is working out perfectly in the perfect time. If you go with the flow, important components to your success will just fall right into place. Feel free to create your own combinations of Switchwords.

You may also use the names of people that you admire or want to be like as a Switchword, thus focusing and lifting your energy. For instance, if you are someone who desires to be a successful author, the name Og Mandino might work for you. If you want to give and receive more love, the names of Jesus or Buddha may work. Of course, you will want to pick the names you connect with; these are only suggestions.

Anytime you find yourself doubting your ability to succeed, say one of these Switchwords or the name of someone you admire over and over until you feel your energy lift. This is another great way of focusing your mind and energy now. As you practice this, you will notice these tools just come to you when needed. They will become a very good habit.

44-DAY
ACTIVATE YOUR
ABUNDANCE PLAN

"The mind is never right but when it is at peace within itself."

---Lucius Annaeus Seneca

Become very present in the *now*. Take the next 10 minutes (at least) and just release everything in your life. All of it is waiting for you when you return from your Divine Meditation, so simply relax. This is just for you, a special time to connect with that Divine part of you that creates miracles. Sit in a chair with your feet connected to the floor or you can actually sit on the ground. This will help to ground you and reinforce your connection. Choose the position that is most comfortable; if you need to lie down, do so. There is no right or wrong way to do this meditation. Take slow deep breaths and relax. Set the intention to connect with your God or higher self. Understand that the word "God" is used to explain this energy that runs through all of us, thus we exist. In case that word is not for you, choose the term that feels best. Words can never adequately define this Divine force and our human minds cannot ever really understand. We can simply allow, be here now and let this Divine energy enhance every area of our life.

Before you start reading and doing your Divine meditations, spend a few moments focusing on all the things you are grateful for in your life. Think about the people you love and how much they mean to you. Think about all you have been blessed with. Appreciation helps to quiet your ego and put you in the perfect state to connect with your inner being. Now let us begin.

Connection

MEDITATION FOR NIGHTS 1 - 4

I am now filled with the ever abundant light of my God. This God force flows through me, thus I am a masterpiece. I now make conscious contact with my God. I bring my mind to the beauty of this moment, thanking the universe that this moment is all I have. I am filled with gratitude that all my power is in the now and I fully enjoy this moment, this peace. I now feel all the love that God flows through and to me in every moment; this knowledge gives me strength and knowing that all things are possible. There is no need to ever worry about where my supply will come from as I relax into the knowledge that my God self supplies everything I need with ease. I now release attachment to any outcome. I release the need for anyone to do anything or be different than they are. I connect back to my power now, my God source. This Divine energy that flows through me is my supply, thus I am blessed and abundant on all levels. My God is never-ending love and all I need to do is remember this and my connection, in order to be filled on all levels. Contentment and satisfaction are mine now. I now let go of the belief that any person, place or thing can supply me. My God-self is my supply. I remember that this Bountiful God is who I *AM*; my awareness of this opens the flow of Abundance *Now*.

Day 1

MAKE THE COMMITMENT TO HAPPINESS

"Happiness is the meaning and the purpose of life, the whole aim and end of human existence."

---Aristotle

Years ago, I heard Marianne Williamson speak about how important it is to make a commitment to happiness. This felt like perfect advice to me. Once we discover that feeling happy will bring peace and more of what we want; we shall want to make feeling good a top priority now.

As we set the intention to feel good now, this mindset brings forth energies that we do not necessarily see but can feel. Helpful coincidences start to become more commonplace. People start pleasing and delighting us in ways we never knew were possible. Life starts to feel better, as if the whole universe is conspiring to make things easier for us. This is the way it is supposed to be, and with a little practice and determination, you will experience your own unique joy. Once we get in this zone, we become enchanted by its rhythm.

Happiness is the ultimate way to attract the abundance we want and deserve. There are stretches when it seems impossible to feel good in the present moment. We are human and all go through

Day 1

periods when it is tough to focus on our blessings, but there are so many things to appreciate, for even the most oppressed person. The trick is to set the intention to fill our mind with Divine Nutrition every day in order to connect with our God-self. First thing in the morning, before we get out of bed, it is a very productive activity to just lie there and count our blessings. Counting our blessings quiets the ego and allows Divine mind to flow in. The fact that we have the eyes to see this and a strong mind to think are just a few of the causes for celebration.

As we focus on all we have in our lives now, we will line up with our God self and allow this Divine energy to accomplish things we could not do on our own. We, by ourselves, can do nothing, but once we line back up with our God-self, we will experience miracles. It is said that we only use 10% of our brains. The way to access the other 90%, our Divine Mind, is to feel good now and set the intention to hear our Divine guidance.

Everyone has different ideas or activities that cause us to align and get happy; it can be anything from reading a funny book, watching an inspiring movie, enjoying the creative process or calling a friend for a fun chat. Use your imagination. You will have your own ideas of what makes you happy; *now* is the time to set the intention to do these things more often. As we start to practice having fun and relaxing, we notice things working out for us more often. We have been told for years that working hard is the key to success. Hard work leads to success if one enjoys it, but it is not the only path to success.

DAY 1

If you are a person who enjoys life at a fun and relaxed pace, you are on the right path. As we understand the laws that govern our ability to line up with our desires, we are on our way. It is empowering to understand that we have already done the work through years of sifting through things we do not want. This has created strong desire in us and we simply need to allow ourselves to line up with these wishes. Ask successful people how they found their way and many say they felt guided or inspired. Now, we simply need to remember that it is enjoying ourselves, relaxing and having faith that leads to all the "coincidences" that line us up with great things. The work is done; now it is time to relax and enjoy the ride more often.

Day 2

BE AS A LITTLE CHILD

"The reluctance to put away childish things may be a requirement of genius."

---Rebecca Pepper Sinkler

Children are incredible examples of living in joy and some of our best teachers. They instinctively know on a deep level that play and having fun are essential parts of an abundant life. Children play and use their imagination often to naturally enjoy what they are doing. As adults we tend to need to be reminded of this from time to time. Let's tap into some of this childhood knowing now.

Go to your favorite place in your mind. Where are you? What time of year is it? Put a smile on your face as you do this; let's get immersed in this experience. Feel how carefree you are, how everything looks so new and pretty. Feel the laughter and joy bubbling up inside of you. Here is the exciting news: when you do this, you are actually lining up and creating the things you want. We are remembering that creating is as natural as breathing; we just need to practice. Now, as you hold this picture in your mind, take a slow, deep breath and remember that all is well; just being present here and now. This is a delicious experience and the more

DAY 2

you bring yourself here, the better you will feel. An important point to note is how easily a child will forget about a problem and just get involved in something else they enjoy. As we take on some of these childlike qualities, we shall experience more peace and bliss.

Day 3

HANDLING NEGATIVE EMOTION

"Dream of your brother's kindnesses instead of dwelling in your dreams on his mistakes."

---A Course In Miracles

Sometimes we attract other people's negative emotions and energy without even being aware of it. For example, we may be enjoying our day and someone will walk in and "give their bad mood to us." Since we are all connected, we sense each other's emotions, especially those we love and are closest to. This is something that once we become conscious of, we want to learn to handle. Remember no one can make us feel anything or "give us a bad mood." We must take responsibility for how we react to others now. We can do this by staying conscious.

I discovered that I used to pick up and take on people's negative energy. Once I understood that this was something I needed help with, I asked God and the Angels for guidance. I was soon given the message that as we become conscious of this, we can use visualization and prayer to help us handle these disharmonious energies. By simply becoming conscious of these negative energies, we can bring light to a situation and start lifting it. Use this visualization whenever you feel uncomfortable for any

DAY 3

reason about someone. See that person in your mind's eye surrounded by white light; take a deep cleansing breath and say: **"I ask God to transform any negative energy between us into Divine Love now." Now see you and this person having positive interactions. Your positive imaginings have much more power than your negative ones.**

You may have to practice this a few times, but as you do, the tight feelings subside and you will know that Divine love is doing its perfect work on the situation now. You will get relief from this process and, with continued practice, the situation will be cleaned up for the best of everyone involved. It is also beneficial to use the tapping technique and other clearing methods such as Ho'oponopono discussed in this book to help clear negative emotions on a regular basis. We will want to see cleaning and clearing our emotions as a personal responsibility and one of the most important habits we can cultivate to enhance our lives.

If we happen to see someone "out of the blue" that we had an "issue" with in the past, this is an opportunity to heal the situation. We may use visualization with anyone that we would like to send love to, in order to heal misunderstandings. The other person does not need to get involved and we do not need to talk to them unless you feel led to. Our Divine visualizations and God energy will create miracles.

Understand, it is God and the Angels doing the work, so we do not take any credit. Simply enjoy the result of much more

DAY 3

loving and fulfilling relationships. As you ask for help, you may be given a much more effective visualization tool. You are unique and shall find the techniques that work best for you. It is asking and setting the intention for things to get better that will bring Divine help. As we become conscious, everything is up for healing and transformation.

Day 4

CLEANING WITH INTENTION

"Being organized is a spiritual process. Chaos is conquered as much by awareness, gratitude, grounding, and breath as by a well-labeled filing system."

---Claire Josephine, The Spiritual Art of Being Organized

Cleaning needs to be understood and given the credit it deserves for being one of the most productive activities we can do. If someone had told me that cleaning with intention creates an amazing life, I would have been much more enthusiastic about it years ago. In the past, like many, I thought housework was just a chore. Now that I understand its Divine ability to create more peace and prosperity, I clean with a proud attitude knowing that I am taking control of my environment and life. There is a Divine power in cleaning and clearing. If you want positive changes in your life, clean it up.

Once we discover that keeping a clean space will bring more of what we want, it takes on a whole new energy. The saying "Cleanliness is next to Godliness" says it all.

If we are experiencing challenges, a great way to feel more empowered is to channel that energy into a good cleaning. I love to

Day 4

put on some uplifting music, relax my mind and just start lifting an area with a vacuum, duster and throwing clutter out. As we clean the area say prayers, positive affirmations or the powerful Switchword combo "Together Divine Order." Here is a wonderful decree to make while cleaning, **"I now ask God and the angels to assist me in removing anything from our home that no longer serves our highest good. I clean with love and knowing that we prosper now."**

Move through your task with the knowing that you are creating more of what you want. This is such an empowering activity.

THE RED ENVELOPE TECHNIQUE

"Life isn't about finding yourself. Life is about creating yourself."

---George Bernard Shaw

Here is another technique that focuses our energy and calls upon Divine assistance. Get a beautiful piece of stationary that says "Abundance to You" and a red envelope. Write out all the things you want to achieve or enjoy in the present "I AM." For example, in the area of relationships (relationship area explained in the section titled "What Is In Your Abundance Area"), you might say:

"I am enjoying fun and healthy relationships; I always find things I love about people."

"I always attract the perfect people at the perfect time."

"I enjoy quality time with my friends and family."

Get more specific with your own. You may want to review the section on imagination to give you more ideas. Now, seal the envelope and place it in your relationship area. Hide it behind pictures or under furniture like a desk -- somewhere only you know. You can now relax in the knowledge that Divine Intelligence is going to work to create more of what you want, as you have used Divine Intention.

Bonus days 1 - 4

Let's create an envelope for the abundance area. Here are some decrees you may use or create your own:

"God is the source and supply of my Unlimited Divine Abundance. I AM successful and happy."

"Anything I need comes easily and effortlessly."

"I have a wonderful career I enjoy where I get to help others and bring in a plentiful income."

Now put your card in your envelope, in a very special place in your abundance area (abundance area explained in the section titled "What Is In Your Abundance Area" Day 6). Use love and intention knowing that Divine Energy is going to work for you.

Setting your intentions with a red envelope in a specific area is very effective. It is always interesting how, when I remember to check on my envelopes later, much of what I have intended has happened, or something better. Try not to get too attached to the outcome; that will block your flow. Just put your desires out there and let it go. Later, you can create a new envelope as your consciousness lifts and your desires evolve. This will help you to identify more clearly what you want and determine if it is for your highest good. The saying "Be careful what you wish for as you might just get it" comes to mind. When you ask for anything, it is good to do so with the intention that only what is for the highest good of everyone involved occurs. This will ensure that

Bonus days 1 - 4

Divine mind and not our human mind is running the show, thus bringing the best.

Many times when we do not get something we really want, after time, it becomes very obvious that this was for the best. For instance, I know many people who had their heart set on a particular mate and things did not work out. When they meet the true love of their lives, they are always relieved that things worked out the way they did. Sometimes we cannot see everything involved and simply need to relax and have faith.

There have been many studies done on the power of writing out your desires to get intended results. Writing desires has been used by conscious creators throughout time with magnificent results; take advantage of this Divine Technique *Now*.

Embrace

By focusing on the fact that God flows through me now, I have access to Divine Intelligence. This God force is available to me by simply feeling good now and remembering who I AM. I AM God's perfect creation, loved by all that is. I feel good now as I remember my Divine birthright to succeed in all things. As I become conscious of the Divine Intelligence flowing through me and available to me at all times, I AM lifted up and proud to be a conscious creator and partner with my God. My work is to relax and stay conscious of this connection between me and my God. This becomes easy as I get still and listen. As I do this, I begin to feel the light of the Divine mind residing within me. I AM part of the God mind now. This gives me the heavenly ability to see things through new and celestial eyes. Everything around me starts to make complete sense and become perfect just the way it is. Nothing needs to change in order for me to be happy and content. I AM blessed and know this now. I AM relaxed in knowing that all my needs are met by this Divine Energy and my struggles are over now.

Day 5

RELEASING BELIEFS THAT DO NOT SERVE US

"Spiritual progress is like detoxification.
Things have to come up in order to be released.
Once we have asked to be healed,
then our unhealed places are forced to the surface."

---Marianne Williamson

A belief is just a practiced pattern of thinking that we call true. We all have unique beliefs. The beliefs that we know to be true are affecting every aspect of our life so it serves us to get our beliefs in line with what we want. For example, if we believe that the world is a safe place, this is reflected back to us on a consistent basis. We are just always at the right place at the right time. If we believe that people in general are good and like us, then we see happy, polite people everywhere we go. **Everything that we are living is a manifestation of the core beliefs and thoughts we hold to be true.**

Understand it is very important for us to make positive beliefs our own. This sounds a little challenging at first, but it is very possible. This book is filled with many helpful ideas for releasing unwanted beliefs. I encourage you to try out the different

DAY 5

uplifting techniques presented and take the best for yourself. Tapping, discussed in the tools section of this book, is one of my personal favorite techniques for releasing unwanted beliefs, emotions and unproductive programs.

How do we know which beliefs serve us well? The beliefs that feel good are going to get us to where we want to be. The beliefs that feel bad when we think about them are the ones we want to lift and release. It is that simple. We can consciously choose a thought that feels a little better in every moment.

With determination and practice we can cultivate beliefs that serve us. Here are some examples:

1) I always find the best in people. People always like me.

2) I always seem to get what I need. I always have everything I need and more. With faith all things are possible.

3) I am always finding fun things to do.

4) I get along great with my mate.

5) I enjoy time with my kids. I am a very successful parent.

6) I always feel great.

7) I love eating healthy foods and exercising.

8) I love and appreciate my body.

DAY 5

Practice these thoughts frequently and just decide that you are going to do so until you believe them, while releasing their negative counterparts. We must clear out the negative beliefs in order to make room for the empowering ones. Releasing negative emotions and thoughts creates a lovely space for what we do want to become. When you become conscious that you are entertaining a negative belief use your EFT, writing it out (discussed ahead) and other techniques to help release it now.

Release your negative stories. When we find ourselves going into a negative story that does not serve us, this is the perfect time to become conscious and release it. Eckhart Tolle reminds us that all these negative stories we tell about ourselves and other people are very problematic. They are the result of our minds being continually grasping. He gives us the perfect tool: simply become conscious of this negative story, stop it and come fully into the present moment.

When we notice ourselves telling a negative story, it is time to become conscious that it is not serving any purpose and stop. As we practice stopping these negative stories, we will be brought immediately into the awareness that it is not serving us. Becoming conscious of these negative stories is a big part of disarming their power. Tolle teaches that our many negative emotions create what is known as a "pain body." This pain body has a life of its own and feeds off our negative emotion. It is common to go on a negative rant about something and not even understand why it is going on. This is a pain body.

DAY 5

As we start paying attention to these pain bodies, thus releasing them, we start to become more conscious and connected to our Divine Source. We also become aware of other people's pain bodies. When we are around someone experiencing a pain body, the most important thing to do is become conscious, calm and non-reactive. If we fight back, it will only feed their pain body and escalate things. Take a deep breath and try some soothing words, letting this person know that everything will be fine; they are simply experiencing some old negative emotions. Of course if you feel guided to get away from this person, do so. Once they "wake up" the whole thing will fade away. I love to say the Switchwords combination "Together Divine Love" to myself anytime I am in a situation that needs some calming. People pick up on our composed mood and everyone benefits.

A very dominant negative belief system running rampant in the collective consciousness right now is distrust and anger toward the opposite sex. This is a heavy subconscious belief system that comes from centuries of oppression and bitterness. As we become conscious and see the problems this is causing in all our relationships, we will want to clear and clean this up. It affects our mates, our children, parents and every relationship we have with the opposite sex.

Many of the programs stuck in our subconscious are of deep distrust and anger toward the opposite sex that manifest in so many unwanted ways. Examples are women being overreactive and aggressive because of unbalanced male female energies. Men

DAY 5

may become closed down or overly aggressive and reactive. Once this deep hurt is addressed, deep healing occurs. I was passed a deep distrust of men that came down through generations too far back to trace. Once I became conscious of this, my main incentive for cleaning up this unproductive belief was my beautiful nephew. As he became a man I realized that these ridiculous stereotypes that society has placed on men and women serves no one. I asked God and the angels to clear this for me. It did not happen overnight, but as it did, miracles occurred.

The biggest miracle for me is now I can clear these false beliefs and avoid passing this to my daughters; it can stop with this generation. The lightness that radiates from our hearts after we get this is a quantum leap in evolution. This awareness is also imperative for men who want to have caring relationships with their daughters. As their little girls become women, these men may adjust with love as these past hurts are cleared. This is groundbreaking and I imagine the benefits of this are endless. As more of us come to understand this over time, it will fill the collective consciousness and create miracles throughout our world. I would say it is time. Our children are so worth it.

As we let go of negative beliefs on a regular basis, we will be given evidence that we are on the right track in the way of positive emotion and feeling really good. These good feelings on the inside will lift our consciousness and start to manifest many fantastic blessings in our world. These gifts come to us as a result of a lifted state of consciousness. A lifted state of consciousness is

DAY 5

the path to abundance on all levels. This is wonderful news! We
have so much power and are lining up with it more ever day.

Day 6

WHAT IS IN YOUR ABUNDANCE AREA?

"Leave the state containing poverty and move into the state containing wealth, and wealth will take on reality. This room has reality and substance because you are thinking from it."

---*Neville Goddard*

The ancient art of Feng Shui (pronounced fung shway) is a science that has been practiced with great success in the Orient for thousands of years. The concept is that you can place certain items in specific areas of your home, business or property with the intention of getting desired results. This is about making the most of the Divine flow of energy in our environment to create more of what we enjoy.

There are different areas of our home that affect different aspects of our life. For instance, stand facing inside the main doorway of your home and point to the far back left corner. This is your abundance area. Go there mentally now. What is in this area? Is it bright, clear and clean? I am giggling because chances are you are shaking your head thinking, "I do not think so," or "This figures." If this area is clean and filled with things you love, good for you. If not, let's create a beautiful space that brings joy to your eyes and life.

Day 6

I am always fascinated by what people have in their abundance area. When a person's abundance area is packed with old broken rusty items and clutter, they are blocked and experiencing challenges. This, however, is easy to remedy with a little enthusiasm and know-how.

One of the first things you will want to do is clean and clear your abundance area. This is the perfect time to clear your clutter.

While you are cleaning, say prayers, affirmations and set the intention for what you would like more of in your life. This is conscious cleaning and very powerful. As you are vacuuming and clearing this area, remind yourself that you are actively creating more of what you want in your life. This gives you a feeling of confidence, more control and cultivates faith. **Raising consciousness needs to be paired with Divine Action. Clearing your clutter is a great place to start with action. This will clear blocks and lead you to the next Divine step, which will feel good. It is conscious and empowering to clear our environment as well as our minds. The two together create the amazing life we deserve.**

Now that this area is clean, it is time for the fun part -- activate it with things that speak to you of abundance and prosperity. This means different things to different people. Some sure bets are big, healthy, growing, green plants with rounded, healthy leaves. Put a beautiful piece of amethyst crystal in the abundance area. Gold coins or anything that resembles money is a

DAY 6

sure bet. Purple is a color associated with enhancing the abundance area, so find something purple you love that signifies prosperity for this area. Speaking of things you love, I suggest you only have things you love in your home. If you do not love it or use it, lose it.

Each room also has its own abundance area. This is where you can really take it to a whole new level. You are activating an area within an area. This sounds tricky but it is really simple and very effective. Like before, simply stand in the doorway facing inside the room you want to activate and look to your back left corner; this is the abundance area of each room.

It is really fun how once we get started, we become more and more comfortable clearing and activating the areas of our home. It just becomes second nature. We walk into a room and know what needs to be spruced up and cleared. Whenever I feel blocked or want something to come to me, I know it is time to clear and give my environment a lift.

Another important area we all want success in is called our love and marriage area. This area affects every relationship in our lives and is really important to keep in tiptop shape. Stand in your front door facing in and point to the far back right corner of your home. This is your love and marriage area. What is in yours? No worries -- if it is not perfect, we are going to explore ways to get this area in great shape.

DAY 6

This area should first be cleaned and cleared of any clutter or dirt, while holding the intention of enhancing all your relationships. Now comes the fun part; we are going to activate it. This area affects our relationships with everyone including our mate, parents, children and friends. It is well worth our time to get this area in order. Start by clearing any dirt or clutter from this area. Now you may place things in this area that say love to you. I, personally, enjoy pictures of couples interacting lovingly. Always place items in pairs; lovebirds are great. If you are looking for a mate, remove any pictures of single men or women. Show couples. A healthy vibrant plant is always a good idea. Crystals and items shaped like hearts are great activators. Try to keep the hearts low key as not to make the area too feminine. A balance of the masculine and feminine energies is productive. Put fresh-cut, beautiful flowers in this area frequently to activate and lift the energy. Do this with intention and say to yourself, **"These flowers are bringing more love and peace to all my relationships; Divine love fills all my relationships now."**

Setting the intention to have better relationships is a very powerful way to improve interactions with people. Set the intention to have more fun with the people in your life. Visualize yourself laughing and playing with them often.

Our consciousness is reflected in our environment, so a clear one is our best bet. The two go hand in hand beautifully. The cleaner and more beautiful our home is, the better we will feel. This will serve us in wonderful ways.

DAY 6

Linda Binns wrote the intuitive book, *Feng Shui for Your Relationships.* Binns gives us a great idea to enhance our lives and relationships: clean and enhance your bedroom first in order to give yourself a boost. I agree with her message that the most important thing we can do to enhance our relationships is practice deep self-love. We must start enhancing the relationship with ourselves first. When anyone is having problems with another, Binns will remind them that we can only change ourselves. **Once we start doing loving things for ourselves, we will start to see the relationships in our lives improve.** She encourages us to work on our bedroom first because this is the room that is closest to us. Create a sanctuary in your bedroom where you love to go and relax. Remove anything that you do not use or love knowing that Divine Intelligence will guide you to the perfect replacement at the perfect time. Make sure to remove any clutter under your bed, as this will improve your sleep. Once our bedroom is cleared and spruced up, we will experience improved results with our self-worth and lives.

It is a fascinating practice to place things in our environment with the intention of enjoying a better life. Is it the Feng Shui creating the blessings or is it because we are using intention? We may never know but one thing is for sure. The things we give our attention to will manifest in our lives. This is why creating beautiful surroundings with intention is such an empowering way to create more abundance in our lives.

Day 7

MEDITATE TO ENHANCE YOUR CONNECTION

"Quiet your mind so that inspirations may rise from its depths. An inflow of new thoughts can remake you regardless of every difficulty you may face, and I repeat –every difficulty."

---Norman Vincent Peale

To make the conscious connection with God through meditation is one of our finest abilities. Meditation is a natural process that quiets our mind and allows Divine wisdom to flow into our experience, creating a lifted consciousness. As we meditate, we unlock forces that create miracles. Our mind becomes an empty vessel to be filled with the wisdom of the ages. The saying "Be still and know that I am God" states the power of meditating perfectly. "I am" reminds us that when we are blended harmoniously with our God energy, we have the answers we seek. There is never any need to seek the answers outside ourselves.

When you meditate, do not get discouraged if you are interrupted. A good friend told me to just think of an interruption during meditation as God saying "hi" and keep with your meditation. You will find your day just flows with a calm and rhythm that only meditation can bring. The Buddha, Jesus and

Day 7

Gandhi were just a few of the geniuses that understood the power of connecting with their God self. They used meditation to connect to their higher power and this allowed them to access Divine information that helped the masses.

When you meditate, do not be frustrated if you cannot stop your thoughts. This is normal! Just let them flow through like waves in the ocean. Your meditation sessions do not need to be perfect to bring peace and blessings.

In Deepak Chopra's enlightening book, *The Ultimate Happiness Prescription*, he states that researchers have confirmed that meditation actually releases hormones in the body that help alleviate depression, enhance self-esteem and pleasure. When you find yourself overwhelmed or not knowing what to do, this is the perfect time to stop, "drop" and meditate. After your meditation session, you will start to remember that everything really is going to be alright. This is because you have allowed your Divine energy to fill your mind, body and spirit.

Set the intention for your meditation sessions to bring more love and peace into your life while making conscious contact with your God. If God is not a good term for you, simply set the intention to connect with that part of you that "knows all." You will find yourself much more centered and steady. You will find that Divine Mind just seems to arrange things in a brilliant manner that no human could achieve on their own. You learn that ease and going with the flow are your strongest allies. This all from sitting at

DAY 7

least ten minutes a day quietly! I would say it is well worth our time.

I want to make it very clear that if a person is experiencing any physical dis-ease, **the most important thing they can do is meditate.** This will help to calm the body, mind and spirit for Divine shifts to occur. This will lead them to the next step that is best for them. It may be a doctor, exercise or nutrition program. Each person is unique and this is why we get such fabulous results when we meditate so we can hear that small, still voice that is speaking brilliantly just to us. No one else has access to it. It is our responsibility to listen. Meditation should be like brushing our teeth, a good habit that we automatically do each day.

Day 8

IT IS ALL ABOUT EASE

"Always leave enough time in your life to do something that makes you happy, satisfied, even joyous. That has more of an effect on economic well-being than any other single factor."

---Paul Hawken

If we are trying too hard to get healthy, better relationships or money, the best course of action is to switch gears and relax. Attracting anything we want should feel like joy and ease. As we bring our higher self into the picture and practice looking for things to appreciate, we will be led on a journey where we line up with things we want more often. We can be assured that these are not coincidences. The better we start to feel and focus on Divine Mind as the source of our supply, the more we will have seemingly miraculous events occur in our life. As time goes on, with our new, uplifted attitude, we come to expect these miracles. A relaxed attitude while expecting great things is the ideal place to create from. When I went through a hard time physically and was looking for a "cure," the more I looked, the more I could not find it. I kept trying my hardest to find a solution. I finally got the message that all I really needed to do was relax. That looking for the "cure" was actually holding me where I did not want to be. It took me a while to get this. When we are sick, it feels like we need to do

DAY 8

something, but once we relax or get distracted, Divine energy can flow in and work its magic. I tell people who want more wellness that meditation and relaxing are truly the "best medicine." I know this sounds too easy and good to be true, but as Abraham-Hicks says, alignment of thought (which is simply put, relaxing and getting happy) is the only thing that ever works and many times a last resort.

If any project or situation feels frustrating or hard, it is time to relax and find a pleasant activity to enjoy. When we come back to what we were doing, we will have a fresh and productive perspective.

WRITING AND TALKING IT OUT

"Above all the grace and the gifts that Christ gives to his beloved is that of overcoming self."

---St. Francis of Assisi

It is human nature to have fearful thoughts from time to time. We are going to become conscious and work on releasing them now, as fearful thoughts create unwanted situations and conditions. "Fear and it will appear." Fearful thinking is a habit that is passed on from parents and picked up from those around us. We will now empower ourselves by becoming conscious of these thoughts and shifting them to something more productive. Releasing and overcoming fearful thoughts takes consistent practice. We all have to work on staying conscious and releasing fear-based thoughts throughout our lives. I personally deal with fearful thoughts and need to practice releasing them regularly. This is part of the reason I am such an avid student of positive thinking techniques and love to share them with others. The good news is we can only hold a fearful thought for so long and then it will have to shift. Be patient and have faith; we can do this!

First, set the intention to release your fears and ask God or your higher-self for assistance. This is a big task and will require Divine assistance. Once we realize that we cannot do this alone and that heavenly help is available, we are on our way.

Bonus days 5 - 8

When we are going through hard or transition periods, many times we need to express our fears in order to clear and work them out. **I am all for positive thinking, but we must be realistic in understanding that it is in our best interest to get old, stuck emotions out of our mind, body and spirit.** We are human, and venting and crying seems to really do the trick.

No amount of "positive thinking" is going to change this. Sometimes we need to vent and just let it out. If left, these negative emotions fester and can lead to problems in our physical well-being and lives. Think of it like needing to remove a splinter in order for a sore place to heal.

We do not want to get stuck in the problem by focusing on it too much, but at times talking or writing it out will bring immense relief.

Ask a friend for permission to talk about this "challenge" with the intention of clearing it out and letting it go. Also set the intention that any negative energy is transmuted into something higher and more loving. If you will be venting negatively about another person, ask that the person's soul is present so that everyone may heal and lift from this conversation. This way you are not just "talking behind someone's back." You are intending solutions for everyone involved. By doing this we are clearing out old, stuck energy patterns and creating room for wonderful, new things to come. This is what Catherine Ponder calls "creating a vortex." You are actually creating a space for fresh new things and can feel really great about what you are doing.

Bonus days 5 - 8

If a friend is not available to listen or it feels too personal to discuss, there is another technique that is very effective in releasing old stale emotions. **Write it out**. Take a piece of paper and write down every negative stressful thought you are having about a person or situation with the intention of clearing it out of your mind, body and spirit. Just keep writing until you feel relief, like a sigh. Let all the hurt and anger out. You may even need to cry -- this is good! Tears and laughter are both so healing. Having a good cry actually releases negative stuck energies and heals the body on many levels. Allow your tears and avoid people who say you should not cry when you need to.

You have a right to your feelings and need to express them. Understanding that you can move on to something much more productive as a result.

Now take the pieces of paper and rip them up, symbolizing this problem leaving you. You now feel a lifting in your heart as old stale negative emotions leave. Every situation is different; you may need to do this many times or once may do the trick. I once went through a period where I had to "write it out" for about a month. I felt better every time I wrote out all the hurt I was experiencing, then all of the sudden it was just gone and I forgot all about it. There is no right or wrong way; simply write it out until you feel relief. For me this is a physical relief, like my heart feels lighter, like a sigh. Again, if you are writing or talking about a person, please do so with the intention of making things better for

Bonus days 5 - 8

everyone involved. Ask that you both learn and get what you are supposed to from this interaction and move on with blessings.

As we consistently release our fears, we feel much better. All things become possible as the blocks to love lift. New doors open and innovative, productive ideas flow into our mind. Situations that once seemed like obstacles appear in a new light. Life becomes more like a game and now the fun can begin.

There is a large part of the collective consciousness where fear dominates. It is our "job" to lift our minds on a regular basis so we do not get caught up in this fearful web. We simply remember that God is always with us and that everything will be alright.

We all deal with fears from time to time, as we are human. Set the intention to stay in a good place mentally and remember how truly safe and loved you are. The 44-day program in this book is a great way to allow the love and release the fear.

Divine Love

Divine Love flows through me now. I AM blessed with this energy and it loves and aligns every part of my mind, body and spirit. Any dis-ease takes care of itself as my Divine mind loves and fills every cell in my body with light. This love is my guiding light and part of who I AM. I call upon this Divine Love to show me the way in every relationship in my life. I no longer need to ask for anything from anyone; God allows everything I need at the perfect time. I can now relax and allow the magnificence that is me. I now consciously become aware that my true nature is that of Divine Love. This Love resides in my heart and mind; I just easily think of it to activate its miraculous powers. I call on it now and know that all things are lifted to a wonderful place. All I do now is focus on this love in order to thrive. It is not my job to fix anyone or anything, only to behold the perfection of Divine Love that exists in everything and everyone now. I now remember that Divine Love is the truth of who I AM.

THIRD EYE RELEASING TECHNIQUE

"Is the Human brain, at some primal level a wondrous computer linked with a universal energy field, that knows far more than it knows it knows?"

---*E. Whalen*

There is another very effective technique I call "third eye releasing." We are going to use the energy meridian of the third eye and strong intention to release. Remember, setting the intention to release a negative emotion actually helps to release it. Simply place your pointer finger over the middle of your forehead when a negative belief or thought occurs. While you are pressing on this point, cradle the back of your head. Now hold the unpleasant thought in your mind while really feeling this thought. Set the intention to release this negative emotion from every part of your body and mind. Say to yourself:

"I now ask God and my angels to help me release this feeling from every cell in my body, mind and spirit. I know at one time I created and resonated with this. I no longer create or resonate with this. I ask to forgive myself or anyone involved. I ask that anyone I hurt forgive me. Once the heavy feeling subsides, see yourself vibrantly happy and abundant. Go into details of how

DAY 9

great things will be now and see things the way you want them. Now, say aloud or to yourself, "I integrate this healing and clearing in all of my mind, body and world now."

You may now release your third eye hold. Take a deep breath and just relax. Take a drink of water. This clears stuck negative emotions very effectively, leaving room for something better. We all have some deep negative emotions that are universal and need to be cleared on. Here are some for us to clear on. You will have your own; listen for them. Examples include:

I am not worthy.

I do not deserve to be happy.

I am not safe.

It is too much work to be healthy and attractive.

I bother people.

People do not have time for me.

There is not enough money to go around.

Also clear on the universal feeling of body shame.

These are just some of the universal fears that are in the collective consciousness. When we notice any bubbling up in us, we can become conscious, clear them and watch our life become more fulfilling. A word about all the releasing techniques presented

Day 9

here. There is no way of knowing how many times we may need to do these in order to feel relief. Just have patience, keep practicing, and know you will feel better soon.

Day 10

TALKING DOWN FEAR

"As we are liberated from our own fear,
our presence automatically liberates others."

---Marianne Williamson

It is human nature to have fearful thoughts. **Fear and worry are our main blocks to love and having the life we desire. I asked a friend once why we all don't love each other more and stay in a happy place. He gave a brilliant answer, "Because we spend that time worrying and in fear." This simple answer had a profound impact on me. I made the conscious decision right then to spend my mind time in love instead of fear as often as possible. We are unable to see these negative programs until we reach a point in our consciousness where we are ready to acknowledge and release them.** This is not easy, but will yield blessings we can only imagine.

As we learn to release and soothe these illusions, we will start to experience deep, satisfying relationships and a fulfilling life. Thoughts are magnetic, so when we think a fearful thought, more thoughts that feel the same will come. This can lead to a lot of stress and anxiety if we do not weed out these fearful thoughts.

DAY 10

Often people will spread fear-based thinking without understanding the consequences. Debating whether these fears are valid is not my intention. Helping us clear them out so we can see a new safe reality is. Talking down and releasing fear is a skill that anyone can acquire with persistence and a little know-how. We are just going to learn to talk to ourselves in a new and much more productive way.

Here is a personal story that will show how releasing fear will benefit a situation. I walk my doggy, Star, every day. It is one of our favorite activities. We have walked together on the same path for years. One day I noticed a very big, scary dog behind a wrought iron fence barking violently at us. All sorts of fearful thoughts started coming to mind. "What if this dog gets out?" and "What if he hurts me or Star?" I entertained all kinds of scary scenarios for about a week. Then, I finally became conscious and decided to talk down these fears. I started saying things to myself like, "He is really just a young dog," "He probably just wants some attention," and "He has a nice family, so he has been raised with love." Then some interesting things started happening. I got up my courage and started saying, "Hi Puppy!" The Divine idea came to me, to bring him a dog cookie and throw it through the fence. I started sending him love and looking forward to seeing him on our walks. A month later, he just disappeared – gone! As I released my fearful thinking and aligned with Divine Mind, there was room for miracles to occur. When we tell a new positive story, the story

DAY 10

changes to more of what we want. My mom always says, "You do not have to change your life, just change your mind."

We simply want to monitor how our gut feels. Fear is actually a physical sensation if we pay attention to it. When these anxious thoughts appear, we feel them in the stomach, heart or throat area. Start by taking a deep breath and becoming conscious. Ask for assistance. Say a decree such as: "I now ask God or my higher-self to help me to clear and release all this fear." This will help to start the process, break up the negative feelings and allow us to move to a softer feeling. We will then want to listen for the ideas and inspirations that come. Refer back to tools like Tapping and Ho'oponopono mentioned earlier in this book. Of course this will take practice, but we can do it.

Once your body realizes that you have found tools to cope with these negative emotions, it will be more likely to let you become aware of deep-seated fears that need to be cleared. If a lot is coming up, this is really a blessing in disguise; releasing these unproductive emotions leads to wonderful peace and happiness. You may also notice physical discomforts becoming less prevalent or disappearing all together. The more we focus on our blessings and deep breathing, the easier it will be. We will start to catch these fearful images early on and allow them to release easier as we become conscious and do the work.

After we identify a negative feeling, the first thing to do is pay attention to our breathing. We are either holding our

DAY 10

breath or breathing shallowly. Simply take a long slow deep breath, pulling the life-giving oxygen deep into your lungs, while affirming our connection to God. Here is a decree to say as we breathe deeply.

"I now remember my Divine Connection to God. I choose to remember how powerful and perfect I am now. I take in Divine Love now."

Oxygen is one of our most powerful tools to soothe the body and mind. Taking in slow, long, deep breaths energizes and fortifies our body. As you pull in these revitalizing breaths, remember your Divinity. Deep breathing connects us back up with our source, the part of us that knows everything is alright. Try it now. Take a full deep breath and feel the sigh of relief from your body. It is said by masters that at the top of every breath, for just a millisecond, there is a flash of joy. Try deep breathing while focusing on your joy now. **Just breathe.**

Day **11**

THE POWER OF RELAXING

"It's not your work to make anything happen. It's your work to dream it and let it happen. Law of Attraction will make it happen. In your joy, you create something, and then you maintain your vibrational harmony with it, and the Universe must find a way to bring it about. That's the promise of Law of Attraction."

---Abraham-Hicks

An intelligent way to fuel our creating power is to fully understand the role relaxing plays in our ability to allow the life we desire. As we relax, we have access to different parts of our brain that serve us beyond anything we can accomplish with effort. This is another reason that meditation is so productive.

Isn't it interesting when people return from a relaxing vacation to find pleasant surprises waiting for them, or they find that the problems they left behind have somehow simply worked themselves out? As we relax and take our minds off the problem, the situation is given the perfect conditions to work out for the best. Taking a break from a tedious project can give us a fresh perspective and lift the project to new levels. Leonardo da Vinci

DAY 11

said, *"Every now and then go away, have a little relaxation. For when you come back to your work, your judgment will be surer, since to remain constantly at work, you lose power of judgment. Go some distance away, because then the work appears smaller and more of it can be taken in at a glance, and a lack of harmony or proportion is more readily seen."*

As we calm our mind, we open ourselves up to new and original ideas that we simply never considered before. Get creative, use your imagination and I know you will discover all kinds of ways to relax right where you are.

Once we understand and harness the power of relaxing to create more of what we want, we will want to strive to become a "master relaxer". Here are some ideas to get us started. I know you will find many wonderful ideas of your own.

Deep breathing is always an effective way to relax. Inhaling oxygen deep in our lungs gives us an immediate sense of well-being. Any time you find yourself stressed, take note of your breathing. You are most likely holding your breath or breathing shallowly. Taking slow, deep breaths connects us to our God-self. As we pull oxygen deep into our lungs, negative thoughts and energy are diffused while fresh air and "light" refreshes us. Visualize your lower belly filling up like a balloon; expand your stomach as far and as full of oxygen as possible. Pull in air deliberately and slowly as you visualize all the tension leaving your body. Now is the perfect moment to see yourself thriving and

DAY 11

feeling better than ever. This is the perfect opportunity to add positive affirmations and beliefs directly into your mind. Here is a lovely affirmation to go with our deep breathing: **"I pull in more love and light with every breath I take. I am open to receive peace and calm now."**

Find wonderful books or movies that relax and take you away. Be very choosy about what you view on TV and use it for the purpose of relaxing and feeling good now. Relax beside a calming body of water and simply take in its entire splendor. Watch a beautiful sunset in a relaxed state of mind, just marveling in the exquisiteness of our blessed earth. Look for soothing background music that is designed to relax and focus you. Music has a 4th dimensional quality in that it has the ability to take us to relaxed and altered states. The tones and vibrations of soothing music will lift our minds, body and spirits. These are just a few ways to relax. I know as you start practicing you will find numerous ways to relax and enjoy your life to the fullest.

DIVINE LOVE SAVES A BUSINESS

"Instead of fighting problems, picture your way out of them"

---Catherine Ponder

In Catherine Ponder's Divine work, *The Prospering Power of Love,* she tells the incredible story of how love brought back a church from difficult times. Ponder was asked to come and work for this church in a leadership position. She explained to the employees that she wanted to use the power of prayer daily to lift the prosperity of the church. Immediately a couple of employees found this idea impractical and left the church. This turned out to be a very good thing, as these individuals were bringing others down. This was Divine Love's first miracle.

One of the other leaders in the church said that this Divine Love Plan sounded good to him and he wanted to participate. Ponder and he spent time together every day in prayer asking that Divine love heal the church. Very quickly they started to notice positive results. People started volunteering to decorate the church and make it much more attractive. The church started prospering financially and attendance went up. This is one of my favorite

DAY 12

stories, as it demonstrates the power of Divine Love to heal a situation.

Once we start to remember how much creative control we have, we can start to direct our thoughts to benefit our lives. We may send love and blessings to lift others. As we allow our minds and hearts to become a vessel for Divine love, we realize that we may direct loving thoughts and prayers to experience blessings.

Bonus
for days 9 - 12

FASTING AND PRAYER

"Pray, and let God worry."

---Martin Luther King, Jr.

One of the most powerful ways to connect with our God and or higher self is to abstain from food for a period of time while actively praying. Fasting combined with prayer has been practiced throughout history with wonderful results. This ancient tool has been lost, so let us rediscover its miraculous benefits here. Fasting and prayer may each be practiced alone with good results, but when practiced together you can expect incredible insights. This is a time when we shall set the intention to be still and really listen for our Divine wisdom. Fasting is another excellent form of clutter clearing. As we empty our bodies and minds of everyday food, we create a space for Divine love and God to flow right in. When we embark on a fast we may expect to feel lighter and clearer. The answers we seek start to flow to us. Paul Bragg, author of *The Miracle of Fasting,* explains that when we fast we actually take pressure off our nerves thus creating more peace and happiness. I find it fascinating that Mahatma Gandhi was well aware of the physical benefits of fasting when he embarked upon his world-changing breaks from food. Benjamin Franklin was quoted as saying, "The best of all medicines is resting and fasting."

When things seem impossible and we do not know what to do, this is the perfect time to embark on a fast combined with

82

prayer. As we start the process of quieting our mind and body from food, we begin to hear that wise inner voice that lies within all of us. Fasting with prayer makes great shifts in our view. We will see things with more clarity and confidence. We get a wonderful feeling of being guided. When things are at their worst this is the perfect time to fast, pray and use the affirmation: **"I do not know what to do and this is alright I have faith that I will be guided to the perfect solutions."**

Questions that seemed impossible before suddenly come into a new light. Life gets easier as we clear the mental and physical clutter. Masters like Jesus, Buddha and Moses knew this and used fasting to create untold miracles. This ancient practice gives us a newfound confidence in ourselves and our ability to connect with our Divine mind. As we clear the body of debris, we clear our channel to receive Divine guidance and love like never before.

I know the idea of missing a few meals may not sound very appealing. As people investigate the power of fasting and prayer for themselves, many find that the temporary sacrifice of food is well worth it for the deep peace and clarity they experience.

I personally suggest juice fasting as the safest, most effective route, but you may want to look at other fasting choices. One of the best guides for juice fasting I have found is *How to keep Slim, Healthy and Young with Juice Fasting* by Dr. Paavo Airola. This book is filled with inspiring stories of how Dr. Airola transformed people with juice fasting, and he gives wonderful

Bonus days 9 - 12

instructions for a successful juice fast. Ultimately you will be led to the best practice for you. As you seek this knowledge, the answers will come; have faith. There is much information available for you to study and then make the best decisions for yourself. Be proactive and seek a fasting path that will enhance your life.

It is said that every thought is a prayer. Now is the perfect time to consciously fast from thinking and speaking negatively of ourselves and others. Let love in to do its Divine healing. During a fast, you may have periods where everything feels upsetting. Simply breathe through this and use one of your helpful tools in this book to ease and clear these emotions. Just realize that this is part of the process as your mind and body clear years of negative debris and emotion. Once the heavy feeling passes, and it does, you will feel a wonderful lightness.

When we fast it is advised that we keep this to ourselves, sharing the experience with our God or higher self only. This keeps us strong and on track. Fasting is not about "showing off," but about creating a deep peaceful space inside to allow for more God energy. When we tell others, this weakens the connection and power of our fast. If people ask you to join in a meal, simply explain that you just ate and are full but will enjoy some lovely conversation with them. Get yourself some water with some lemon if available and enjoy this person on a whole new level, without the distractions of food.

Fasting and praying for another person is one of the most empowering activities we can embark upon. If a friend or family

84

Bonus days 9 - 12

member is in need, this is the perfect time to fast and pray for them. You will be amazed as your connection to Divine energy gives you clarity on the situation. Fasters become a strong channel for Divine love and intelligence to flow through. Fasting and prayer help us to release fear and gain a better perspective. You will understand things in a new positive light. When someone needs our help, we can do this best from a place of feeling good ourselves. Getting upset and scared for another actually makes things worse. The most effective way to help others is to lift ourselves and become a strong example. The strength we obtain from a fast with prayer is beyond compare. Once you have had a successful fast with prayer, you will understand the power. Others will see and feel your strength and be lifted as a result.

When you decide to try your first fast (after studying and finding the best one for you), be easy on yourself. Many times I try to start a fast day after day without success. Then all of the sudden my body and mind will just do it and have the perfect fasting experience. Just keep trying with faith and know it will work out at the perfect time. Once you embark on your fasting journey, you have a magnificent tool that you may use to enhance and heal your life when you need it.

Blessings

I AM open to receive all the blessings and abundance that are always flowing to me now. I now become aware that there is more than enough for everyone and I unlock the all mighty power of my God by remembering my connection and divinity now. I AM the Greatest Miracle in the world. I AM blessed with the eyes to see this, the mind to understand this, the lungs to take deep breaths and many other blessings too numerous to count. I now become aware of all the plentiful miracles that I have taken for granted for far too long. I now thank God every day for all that has been bestowed upon me. I now remember that I have a vast supply flowing to me and all I need to do is open the flood gates with my powerful knowing that God resides within me and provides all. I AM now releasing any negative thoughts or beliefs that could keep me from my good. I release any thoughts of limitation, scarcity or criticism. I ask that God and my angels help me release these limiting thoughts, for I know I need Divine help with this. I ask God and my angels to help me day and night to think higher loving thoughts that serve me and everyone around me. I AM lifted and renewed by seeing through Divine eyes. I See the Light!

Day 13

QUESTIONING OUR NEGATIVE THOUGHTS

"Even if our efforts of attention seem for years to be producing no result, one day a light that is in exact proportion to them will flood the soul."

---Simon Weil

Paying attention to what we focus on and letting go of anything that does not feel good is a valuable skill we want to cultivate. **When something feels bad to think about, this is a "hot spot," creating things we do not want and needs to be cleared.** Ask yourself, "Is this train of thought worth following?" If not, what are some more constructive thoughts I can replace this with? Releasing negative thoughts can be done many different ways and everyone has unique systems that work for them.

Byron Katie, author of *Loving What Is,* created what is known as "the work." I love her work, in that it is very effective in helping us understand that our negative thoughts are not real; they are just thoughts and have no power over us unless we believe them. Her book, *Loving What Is*, explains this concept in detail. She teaches us to question our negative thoughts so we can

DAY 13

understand that they are just thoughts and only have the power we give them. As we start to become conscious, we can relax and see these negative emotions for what they really are: thoughts that need love and adjustment.

Once we become conscious of a negative thought, she reminds us to question it by simply asking, "Is that true? Can I be absolutely sure that this negative thought is true?" This will start the process of allowing these thoughts to "release us."

For example, a person may have the thought that they are never happy. They would question this by saying "Is that true that I am never happy?" Then sit with that question for a minute and think about it. Even meditate on it, if necessary. As they think about this, they may start to realize that this negative thought is not true. In fact, there are moments when they are happy; they have just gotten in the habit of focusing on the times they are not and giving that too much attention. This process asks a person to give a yes or no answer. Going into any excuses or a story about why they are never happy interferes with the process. A simple yes or no answer is required; it cuts the thought off and shows it up for the misperception it is. If we do not go into our "stories" about how "bad" things are, then the thought loses its steam. After sitting with this for a minute, if a person is still holding onto the negative thought, again the question is asked, "Can I be absolutely sure that I am never happy?" The fact that they cannot give a definite "Yes" makes it obvious that sometimes they are happy.

DAY 13

Katie explains that questioning our negative thoughts actually allows the "thoughts to release us." This is easier than "us releasing the negative thoughts" in that we do not need to do anything, the negative thought will just lighten as a result of Katie's simple but effective questions.

The next question is, "What would my life be like if I could not think this negative thought?" This question makes it more obvious that this thought pattern is not serving, that without this thought we could relax and enjoy life more. Imagine if, all the sudden, we could not think this negative thought anymore. What a relief that would be!

Let us look at a common negative thought pattern: "People do not respect me." If we have this negative thought pattern stuck playing in our head, you can imagine that it is creating many unwanted things. Even if we have people say some nice things to us, we will not be able to believe the compliments because we have gotten so attached to the negative thought pattern that says, "People do not respect me."

Now, just think how freeing it would be if we could no longer hold that negative thought. When people came up to compliment us, we would receive it with love and even come to expect compliments, thus attracting more. **I am a firm believer that it is up to us to focus on the things we want to see more of from people. The more we focus on the things we like about people the more they will show these wonderful qualities to us.**

DAY 13

Complaining about what others "do to us" is only creating more of the unwanted behavior. **Blame is not really going to get us too far.** It is so important to learn to look within, clean up our own thinking and allow the miracles to flow into our lives. This is true empowerment. I know when we are going through difficult periods with others, it feels very hard to shift. As we take full responsibility for our relationships we are back in our power. If we look to others to "make us happy," we will be caught in a trap. Once we understand that our happiness is our responsibility, then we are in our power. When we get confused and say that "someone is making us unhappy," we have unknowingly given them all our power. I want to remind you that no one can make you feel anything. Remember the power to make us happy comes from within and our connection to Divine energy.

Byron Katie tells the story of a man who started using her process of questioning his negative thoughts. He happened to go on a business trip when he started using Katie's method, so changes were taking place while he was away from his family. He returned home two weeks later and noticed that everyone in his household was "bending over backwards to please him." When he asked his wife why everyone was being so nice to him, she said, "I do not know what you are talking about. We are not trying to please you; it is you who has become so pleasant." **This is one of the most powerful secrets to a successful life. Asking circumstances and people to change in order to make us happy is a waste of time. The trick is to get happy and then all the**

DAY 13

situations and people in our life will fall into place to "magically" please us. Try doing "The work" in the privacy of your own mind.

Day 14

CULTIVATING DIVINE ATTITUDE

"Just as light brightens darkness, discovering inner fulfillment can eliminate any disorder or discomfort. This is truly the key to creating balance and harmony in everything you do."

---Deepak Chopra

It takes a strong determination to focus on what we want without getting caught up in what is going on around us. There is so much in this day and time to distract and take us from our peace: the job, the bills, the kids, the parents, the employers, the employees, the mate. This can all get overwhelming at times, pulling us away from that still inner knowing. We want to stay conscious and cultivate being in the *now*; we are the determining factor. This is what the saying "being in this world but not of this world" means. As we take our attention off the things of this world and remember how to go within and feel the invincibility of Divine mind, all things become possible. This means, regardless of what is going on around us, we want to remember that feeling good is an inside job. We cannot find this peace outside of ourselves. There is not a house big enough or a mate perfect enough to give us peace because the mind will always keep reaching for more. How many times have we gone after something because we knew it would make us happy? Then once we got it, we were looking around for

DAY 14

the next thing. This is where being conscious will serve us. We can become aware of this grasping nature of the mind and practice meditation and appreciation to still this anxious behavior. True abundance is about being happy with what we have and being open to receive.

A Divine attitude remembers that if we allow Divine Wisdom to steer the boat, we may sit back and enjoy the ride. All the years of struggle have served us in countless ways, thus we may bless them and relax now. Of course the grasping mind says, "Whoa, you cannot relax, things might fall apart." This is when you will simply become conscious of this negative thought form so you may soothe and release it. Seeing that thought for the fear-based idea it is will help. Just be with it and allow it to dissipate in its own time. Here is a decree to help:

"I now remember that Divine intelligence flows through me. I release the need to struggle or change anything. I simply allow and appreciate all my blessings."

This is our God mind and we may connect to it any time we desire. Simply become conscious and ask. As we do this, feelings of peace and joy will spread.

THE FEELING PLACE

"I tell you that imagination creates reality and I ask you to imagine a state, any state, which would imply the fulfillment of your desire."

---Neville Goddard

As we work with our imagination, it is important to understand that a big part of this process is getting to that place that feels really delicious. For instance, picture yourself laughing so hard you cannot speak; now hold that feeling as long as you can. Twenty seconds is good, longer is great. As you are holding that laughing picture, let the smile flow to your face; see another person you love with you laughing so hard that tears are running down their cheeks. The two of you are smiling at each other in total bliss. Are you there? Feel it? Yes, that is the place. Now, you know you can get there anytime, so come back often for "bliss breaks." You can do this. It has been proven that looking at pictures of smiling people will actually lift our mood. Smiling actually affects your mood for the better. So smile for no reason and feel the small shift for the better and allow it to become so much more.

DAY 15

Another vision that may inspire you is to see yourself glowing with beauty and vitality. Your hair is flowing and a beautiful, vibrant color. Your body is toned and healthy. Your muscles are defined to perfection. You have a powerful look of knowing on your face, like you can do anything you want. You are fully in your power now. You are wearing the finest clothing that enhances your attractiveness. You are like a magnet drawing all wanted things, people and circumstances to you. See it and notice how empowering it feels. Look out, fiction writers; we may be getting ready to give you a run for your money. Our positive imagination is thriving now and flows over into every area of our life if we allow and use it on a consistent basis.

How we feel determines what is coming to us, so it is a good idea to pay attention to this now. We do not want to get scared of our thoughts but rather to be gently guided into enjoying this powerful now. This moment is all we have, so why squander it worrying about the past, present or future? When we are in joy, appreciation and love now, this is the perfect place to attract things that will bring us more of the same feelings. We are attracting, much like a radio antenna brings music from a radio station. Our feelings and emotions are the indicators of what we are bringing to ourselves. It does not serve us to be frightened of our negative emotions as they are guidance, letting us know to choose thoughts that feel a little better. Our emotions should be taken full advantage of. There is no need to monitor every thought; we shall simply set

DAY 15

the intention to feel good now. This will line us up with more peace, love and well-being.

Understand our goal is to get to the feeling place of already having everything we want. Imagine what it is like to be this person we are becoming. Feel the confidence, contentment and knowing that you are the master of your own destiny, that you will always have everything you need and more, that you are aligning with everything that you desire. When we are peaceful and appreciating, we are in the perfect state of mind to allow Divine Energy to manifest in our life. This takes practice, but we can do it; we must be dogmatic. We must be like the saying "a dog with a bone." Set the intention to stay in a good place mentally and be determined.

As we do this more and more, we will be given evidence that we are on the right track. We are allowing this God Energy to flow through us and it is becoming what we desire around us. Little "coincidences" start occurring that please us. Make no mistake; these are not coincidences but alignment of our God energy manifesting more of what we want. Once you have experienced this serendipity for yourself, you are hooked. The more you practice feeling good, the better your life will get; the better your life gets, the more you are inspired to reach for that happy feeling place.

It is up to us to focus on the parts of our life, people and situations that we want to see more of. Pay attention to how you

Day 15

are feeling. If we notice negative emotions running rampant in our mind, it is time to become very aware of the mental pictures we are creating. Are they good pictures? Would you want these things to come into being? If not, be diligent about changing them to pictures that make you happy and bring you peace. Stop and become conscious, pulling yourself into this perfect moment. It helps to take a deep breath and remind ourselves that we are safe here and now. This conscious mindset will break up the negative energy around our worry. When it feels like we cannot calm our thoughts, this is the perfect time to meditate and let our Divine Mind come in.

Test these techniques out for yourself and experience your God-self. Once you have tasted this sweet feeling of connection, nothing else will do. You may fall away from it from time to time, but just know that you can always find your way back to the peace of mind and happiness that is your birthright. With this incredible mindset, the abundance of peace, love and joy will begin to flow. Some days it will be simpler than others, but we have our own personal guidance system in the way of our emotions. When we feel good, we are on the right track. It really is that simple!

Day 16

MAKING THE DIVINE CONNECTION

"God is to me that creative Force behind and in the universe, who manifests Himself as energy, as life, as order, as beauty, as thought, as conscience, as love."

---Henry Sloane Coffin

We are going to remember that connecting to our Divine Intelligence is how we create and live the life we desire. There is no right or wrong way to do this. Simply set the intention and be guided. I know this sounds vague, but you will be given direction; have faith. Remember faith opens the communication between you and the Divine. This is why faith is spoken of reverently throughout time.

Divine Energy has been given many names. This is the energy that created us and this beautiful world. This energy spoke through Jesus, Buddha, Moses and many other amazing individuals. This Divine Energy flows through us all the time; thus, we exist.

The most important point for us to understand and use to our advantage is that the more loving and happy we are, the more this Divine Energy flows through, helping us to create and enjoy more of what we desire. Feelings of resentment, anger, jealousy

DAY 16

and despair are part of life, as we are all human, but need to be understood for exactly what they do. These negative emotions alert us that we are slowing God Energy from flowing freely through us. Negative emotion is a sign that Divine God Energy is getting blocked by unproductive thoughts. These emotions are our road map. We shall pay attention to how we feel so we can be guided.

When we feel joy and love, we are thinking thoughts that will serve us. **When we feel negative emotions, it is time to lift our thoughts. This is our most important work.** When we have negative emotions, there is no reason to be hard on ourselves, for we are all human. Our best course of action is to just feel the negative emotion and move through at our own pace. **If we judge ourselves and push against the negative emotion, we are holding it to us. Accept your emotions and they will lift at the perfect time, understanding that they serve us on many levels. I mean if we never have a sad experience, how can we truly appreciate the beauty of a happy time? Trying to see the beauty in all situations and people is who we truly are. We are so much more than we give ourselves credit for.**

Think of yourself as an electrical being that needs to be a clear channel for God Energy. Love, joy, faith and similar thoughts clear this channel and keep it open to Divine wisdom.

Anyone who has ever created anything magnificent in this world did it from a place of true connection to their God and Divine Wisdom. The good news is that we all have access

DAY 16

to this Divine Blessed Connection 24 hours a day, 7 days a week. All we do is focus and strive for the thoughts that feel a little better. We want to remember that we will have disconnected moments and appreciate them, knowing we shall return to our peace at the perfect moment.

As you start to feel the peace, joy and serenity that come from making this connection though consciously uplifting your thinking along with your 44-day program, you will know you are on the right track. This is something we shall practice on a regular basis for the rest of our life. Of course, there will be days that are easier than others, but as we make Divine connection our goal, we joyfully reap untold benefits.

ACKNOWLEDGE YOUR PERFECTION

"You have been told that you are a special piece of work, noble in reason, infinite in faculties, express and admirable in form and moving, like an angel in action, like a God in apprehension."

---*Og Mandino, The God Memorandum*

Appreciating what we have and where we are in life is a prospering quality. Our real power is in the now and in learning to appreciate what we do have. Og Mandino wrote *The God Memorandum*. This little powerhouse of a book changed it all for me and has helped millions of people. One of its simple messages is "to appreciate what we have in order to experience Divine mental states." Og Mandino reminds us that we are blessed with the eyes to read this; this alone is great cause for celebration and appreciation. He gives us an inspiring list of blessings that each and every one of us has to appreciate now. He discusses simple things that we have many times taken for granted, like our wonderful hearts that constantly beat for us, our amazing lungs which are constantly working for us and many more blessings. Mandino asks us to read *The God Memorandum* for 100 consecutive nights in order to get amazing lifts in our consciousness.

Bonus days 13 - 16

I received such miracle results from reading *The God Memorandum* that it helped to inspire the 44-day program in this book. Lifting our consciousness on a consistent basis adds to a wonderful mindset and an abundant life. **When we stay in appreciation, we are becoming a magnet for our good to come to us.**

Take the time to look for the things about your life you love; this is our most important work. As you continue on your 44-day *Activate Your Abundance* Program, pay attention to how the nightly meditations encourage you to look for and to appreciate all your blessings. This is a key component to our success. When we are focused on all the magnificent abundance around us, it naturally puts us in a Divine state. This is the place from which to create. This is being in our God-power. We all have access to this connection and need only to become conscious in the moment to tap into this Divine state of mind.

Consciousness

I now release the desire to control or manipulate any person or situation. I choose to allow Love's Divine energy to flow into every situation in my life, giving it the perfect balance. I now remember that in me resides a higher power that is all knowing, all seeing and recognizes the best and brightest possible outcomes for my life now. I now release control to God or Divine Intelligence with complete confidence that all things will work out better than I could have ever imagined. I practice remembering that God and Divine Order flow through me and, as a result, I have access to the most miraculous of circumstances. I allow Divine Love to flow into my life and uplift all areas. I know that even if outward appearances are not what I want, Divine Intelligence is putting all things in Divine Order and I need only wait on the Lord. I will simply get quiet and wait with faith for the miracles to occur as God fills my mind, body and life with the perfection that is God; that is me. This is the meaning of the statement, "I AM that I AM." All my years of struggle and trying to control things are over now. I simply sit back and call upon this wisdom deep within me, to do all that needs to be done. I enjoy watching as Divine Intelligence creates the highest good for me and for everyone involved. I remember we are all one.

CLEARING OUR BLOCKS TO LOVE

"While we like to think that all of our unspoken thoughts are private and that they are confined to our own heads, it's not true."
---*Dr. Bradley Nelson, The Emotion Code*

In relationships, there are always things that we want to change about other people. It is exhausting and a waste of time to try to change others. Remember we are all very connected and pick up on each other's thoughts. Explaining things once is healthy and constructive. Constantly complaining will never get us the results we desire. By nagging and focusing on the negative behavior, we are actually creating more of it. **We spend years looking to others for love, then pick apart the love they give us. Children do not do this; it is a learned behavior taught by adults. We all have the ability to become conscious in this moment and love ourselves and others like never before.** It is time to take full responsibility for our relationships. We can do the work of clearing and loving ourselves to become the person we are looking for.

Here is a technique that will create better relationships: First, set the intention for a loving, harmonious relationship. Ask God or your higher-self for help; they can only help when asked. Have a loving conversation with this person in your head and visualize the two of you agreeing and getting along beautifully.

DAY 17

This is in no way a means to control or to manipulate another. This is positive visualization and training our minds to focus on what we desire. Ask that things work out for the highest good of everyone involved in the situation.

Also, be unattached to the outcome. There is a Divine intelligence at work here that can bring things in wonderful ways that we never dreamed of. **If we have our ideas about how things should work out, we are blocking this Divine flow and missing out on all kinds of great things.**

Next, it is important to ask God or our higher-self to help us release all our blocks and self-defeating old programs to love. We have so many we cannot see. It is so simple to see them in others, not so easy to see them in ourselves. We look at all the things others are doing wrong, in complete denial of our role in the situation. Our work is to be open to what comes when we ask for help and do the work to clear it. I personally have spent years picking at my beautiful, perfect husband. A dear friend helped me to see this and change this deeply destructive behavior. I now know that he is one of my greatest teachers and merely a reflection of me. **The things we find most unattractive in others are things we actually do not want to face in ourselves -- a form of denial. Sound familiar? We all do this.**

It is said by psychologist that our need for love and approval is as strong as our need for food. Please take this into

DAY 17

consideration and be easy on yourself knowing we are all doing the best we can in every moment.

When we are ready, we can become conscious and clear these blocks and old programs to experience deep self-love and grand relationships with others. The fascinating thing is that as we clean up the relationship with ourselves, as a result, all of our other relationships shift for the better or disappear. The people that are not for our highest good will leave; do not fight this, as it is creating room for wonderful blessings. As you make the effort to love yourself and others just like they are, you will be creating the life you desire. This is so worth our time to work on. The beautiful thing is we can do this anytime in the privacy of our own minds. A strong desire, open mind and heart are all that are needed. Remember not to get too attached to the outcomes. Just let Divine energy do its work through you.

There is a classic fable about a peasant who is so focused on how he wants things to be that he misses out on the opportunity of a lifetime. This peasant lives in a village with his family and they barely get by every day. A terrible flood comes to his village and things get even worse. The man must walk many miles to town every day to find work to feed his family. On the way to town, his feet get many cuts because he has no shoes. Walking (moving forward in life) becomes very painful.

Once he finally gets to town, he sees some beautiful boots in a cobbler's window. He starts dreaming about how easy his life

DAY 17

would be if only he had these boots. He prays and prays for God to give him these sturdy boots.

One day on the way to town, the peasant hears a young man yelling for help. The boy had fallen in a lake and could not swim. Without thinking the peasant jumps in the water and saves the boys life. The boy's father is a very wealthy **"Lord"** and asks the peasant to a tavern for lunch to show his appreciation. The wealthy **"Lord"** offers to reward the peasant with anything he desires. The peasant immediately sees the shoes in his mind and starts getting very excited, telling the **"Lord"** all about the shoes in the cobbler's window. The **"Lord"** tries to speak but the peasant is so excited he cannot stop talking about how much these shoes would help him and his family. Finally, the wealthy **"Lord"** gives up trying to speak and takes the peasant to get the shoes.

The peasant is filled with glee, thanks the **"Lord"** and runs all the way home to tell his family of his good fortune.

After the peasant leaves, the **"Lord"** looks at his son and says, "How odd, I would have given him anything he desired: a lifetime supply of gold, a beautiful home, anything, but all he could think about were those shoes."

This story clearly illustrates how we block much of our abundance by getting too attached to how and what things should come to us. Enjoy the moment and be open to all the good that is on its way. This mindset will result in wonderful blessings. Our limited human mind cannot compare to the grandeur that the

DAY 17

Divine Mind can bring us. The phrase "Let go and let God" says it all.

Another powerful mind technique we all benefit from is learning to see others in their power. When a loved one is going through a difficult time, the most loving and beneficial thing we can do for them is to visualize them thriving and in their power. This is not always easy, but with intention and vision, we can do it. I personally find this is much easier if we give this person some space to be. As we visualize them thriving, this helps them on many different levels. We are sending a strong positive signal that can help to light their way during dark times. I always tell friends or family who are struggling, **"I see you as whole and perfect, everything is working out for the best of everyone involved."** They can feel this confidence and knowing. We are best equipped to help our loved ones when we ourselves are steady and strong. Getting upset takes us out of our power and does not help anyone. We are all human and will get disconnected at times; just know that we can return to our peace and place of power as we become conscious.

Day 18

UNDERSTANDING ANOTHER PERSONS ANGER

"Holding on to anger is like grasping a hot coal with the intent of throwing it at someone else; you are the one who gets burned."

---Buddha

It is helpful to understand that when another person acts negatively or angry with us, it is really a call for love. Anger is a self survival mechanism. The angry person is doing the best they can -- but do not take on their anger! This is a time when it pays for us to become very conscious. It is human nature to want to "attack" them back. We are once again going for the mindset and action that will serve us best and keep us in our power. A great affirmation to say is: **"I stay in my power regardless of what others do around me. I do this by connecting to my source now."**

I do want to add that anger has its place, and when we need to express anger, we should allow ourselves this emotion and not feel guilty about it. **The goal is to take our anger out at the gym or punch a pillow. Remain conscious enough to avoid taking it out on another person.** Fear leads to dis-ease and depression. Anger again is a self survival mechanism. Feeling angry is much

DAY 18

more empowering than the helpless feeling of depression. It is a "taking back of our power." I explain this in detail in my first book, *How Green Smoothies Saved My Life.*

Realizing that another person's anger does not have to affect us is part of becoming conscious. They are upset, angry with themselves and projecting it onto us. We need to ground ourselves in love and radiate it. Of course, you can do this from a distance. If you feel the urge to get away from a person, listen to your guidance and do so.

Here is something to consider from Dr. Bradley Nelson, author of *The Emotion Code:* **"Suppose you have a trapped emotion of anger. You've carried it around for years, not even knowing it was there. As a result, whenever you come into a situation where you *could* become angry, it's much more likely that you *will* become angry, because in a fascinating and literal way, part of you is *already* angry."** Nelson goes on to explain that these trapped emotions are like tuning forks. When a tuning fork is struck, it makes all the other tuning forks around it resonate to the same sound frequency. This is what happens with people. If a person walks into a room carrying the strong vibration of anger, this will start putting out a signal that can bring others who are not conscious into that anger. Have you ever noticed an angry person come into a situation and just make things worse and everyone around them angry?

DAY 18

As we clear this in ourselves, we are much less likely to become angry. I, personally, experienced the trapped emotion of anger for years. When I used the clearing techniques in this book with the powerful intention to release the vibration of anger from my body, untold miracles occurred. I was changed and healed in profound ways. You will want to work on releasing anger or any other trapped negative emotion from your body for deep feelings of peace and contentment. You will be given many tools. This does not mean that I never get angry, as sometimes just venting and clearing the air will give huge positive shifts, but by clearing anger, we can stay conscious and go into it less often.

My daughter taught me the biggest lesson on anger. Once, I was in an irritable mood and I behaved with anger around her. After I got my balance back, I said, "I am sorry I acted so rudely; you know my anger has nothing to do with you." She just shrugged her shoulders and said, "No biggie."

I was amazed at this relaxed attitude and wanted to know more. I said to her, "Sometimes when you act angry with me it makes me feel bad." (Of course no one can make me feel bad, I do that myself.) How do you keep it from bothering you?" She said, "Even when you get mad, I still know you love me and I love you."

I sat in awe just taking in what she had said. The truth of her statement rolled over and changed me forever. Sometimes when we are experiencing someone else's anger, it feels so real and

DAY 18

like we have done something wrong. Becoming a conscious observer of this allows us to see that this is just a fleeting moment and has no bearing unless we focus on it. We are human and we are going to go into anger at times. Others will also get angry with us. As we become more conscious, it is infinitely wiser to allow anger on either side to run its course and then move on with love. We all have such heavy expectations of each other. The urge to judge and hold a grudge when someone has been angry with us is natural. Now is the time to understand that everyone really is doing the best they can. Being angry with someone for getting mad is not going to help anyone. Just allowing others to be as they are puts us in a wonderful place. As we learn to accept people as they are, we will find peace and be accepted for who we are more often.

Having patience and sending love will benefit all. I am not saying it is our job to soothe others; I am saying it is in our best interest to stay connected to love, our place of power. The more we send love, the less we will find ourselves around angry people, because we are also cleaning up our own issues.

This is the perfect time to say our Ho'opoopono prayer to ourselves. When we have been practicing our powerful processes, they will automatically come to us when we need them.

We may also use Switchwords to help soothe anger. Saying "Together Divine Love" to ourselves over and over is very calming to us and those around us. We do not need to say it aloud; the

DAY 18

people around us will feel this loving energy and respond positively.

I will never forget the first time I discovered the power of Switchwords to soothe situations. I walked into my daughter's school. There was a very big project due from all the kids and everyone was visibly nervous. I thought this might be a great time to try out the Switchwords "Together Divine Love." As I started saying the words to myself, I felt as if a bubble of calm came over me. I remember thinking "Wow, is this my imagination?" At that moment a teacher looked at me and said "Hi, so nice to see you." We both smiled and I knew that I was radiating a calm, loving presence with my Switchwords. I was hooked.

The Dalai Lama came to my city. I did not know a lot about him but felt compelled to go see him. He is magnificent and radiates a calm and loving energy that touches everyone he meets. I could not hear or understand a lot of what he said, but it did not matter. I received a wonderful message of love and peace that I could actually feel. He has an amazing energy that radiated and shifted me for the better. He obviously radiates love and compassion. I could then take this energy out and share it with everyone around me; this is how it works. As we lift ourselves with love and happiness, it naturally enhances the people around us. I am not saying it is our responsibility to take care of others; it will just happen automatically. When we raise our consciousness, we are lifting everyone around us.

Day 19

BE HAPPY FOR OTHER'S SUCCESS

*"If I choose to bless another person,
I will always end up feeling more blessed."*

--- Marianne Williamson

Everyone has had the experience of feeling jealous of another person's success at one point in time. Let us lift to our Divine nature to understand this. There is a constructive way to view jealousy. We simply need to understand that this person is giving us a wonderful gift -- if only we allow it! They are showing us something we want that in this moment we do not believe we can have. We must remember that as we allow Divine mind to flow to us, we will receive ideas that prosper and line us up with what we are wanting. Jealousy is one of those emotions that reminds us we are blocking our good. It is in our best interest to become conscious and work on clearing it. With faith, we can come into a peaceful expectant place. We can become conscious that it is good to want things and be happy for other's success. **Wanting while in positive expectation is a powerful place to create from.**

DAY 19

Let's now come to understand the power in being happy for others when they are doing well. First, as we practice feeling happy for others, it creates a strong God Energy that magnetizes everything that is good to us. That is enough for me, but there is more. Successful people pick up on this and they begin to radiate to us. As we start hanging around successful people, we naturally become more successful; this is law.

It is common to see another person prospering and notice that little negative voice in our head making comments like "Why don't I have that big house?" or "Why don't I have an attractive mate?" Take action now and tell that little voice, "Thank you for sharing, but I am happy for them, they deserve that." Catherine Ponder has a perfect statement she makes for just such an occasion, **"What God does for others, he does for me now and more."** The habit of blessing others' success will ultimately lift us to a very prosperous consciousness. Be easy on yourself; we are all human. As we remember that there is plenty for all, we will run right into our abundance.

Day 20

JUDGE NOT

"If you judge people, you have no time to love them."

---Mother Teresa

It is human nature to judge others harshly at times, but it does not serve us. We want to clean up this unproductive thinking in order to thrive in all areas. If we become conscious and start looking for the things we love about others, this brings us immense peace and blessings. I love Elizabeth Barrett Browning's beautiful words, "How do I love thee? Let me count the ways." If we really think about this, it is perfect thinking, to actively look for things we love about another. What blessings this will bring.

Judging others comes from a place of deep insecurity. We believe that if we make others wrong, it somehow makes us better. This is a natural human tendency that needs to be cleared with Divine intention and all our releasing tools. Judging is a trapped negative emotion that is causing problems we are not aware of. We can release it and experience Divine mental states.

Judging creates negative situations in our lives we do not want, anything from unpleasant interactions with people to health issues or unwanted financial situations. For example, if a person is

DAY 20

harsh or critical of another, they will find others responding negatively to them when they are looking for support. **It is law -- what we put out there comes back to us over and over again.**

It is in our best interest to become very aware and remove the habit of negatively judging. This takes practice, but *We Can Do It*! Again, this is about being aware of our thoughts. We may use the tapping and releasing techniques in this book to help release these negative thoughts. We shall want to pay close attention to the behaviors that we are criticizing, realizing that as we clear these judgments in ourselves, we are creating space for wonderful, new thoughts and things to come to us. It is also important to understand that when we judge things harshly, we are setting ourselves up to deal with similar situations in order to learn and develop compassion. Sooner or later, the things we judge will come home to nest.

Next time we get the urge to judge someone negatively, we need to pay attention and say to ourselves, "I refuse to entertain these negative thoughts one more minute." Then, start tapping on them. Our goal is to just "let it go" and move on to something desired. Here is a Divine Decree that will help us to soften judgmental energy and relax a bit. Take a deep breath and say:

"Dear Lord, I now ask you to help me see this person or situation as you do. I know that I do not understand all that is going on here. I want to free myself of this critical feeling and replace it with Love and Peace, thus I am blessed."

DAY 20

This is advanced love thinking, so we must go at our own pace and never make ourselves wrong for judging. As we find ourselves stopping a negative judgment in the middle, we feel lighter and know we are on the right track. As we become better at just allowing others to be as they are, we will find ourselves being accepted as we are more often.

 *Bonus*

THE POWER OF SMALL GROUPS

"Never doubt that a small group of thoughtful, committed people can change the world. Indeed, it is the only thing that ever has."

---Margaret Meade

When two or more are gathered with Divine Intention, we can expect miraculous shifts in consciousness and situations. Years ago, I read about the power of small groups for creating success. I did not have a lot of "like minds" around me and really wanted some. I started praying for direction and was lead to many ways we can do this. One of my favorite ideas for creating a small group is simply sending and receiving positive uplifting texts, e-mails or letters to friends. They, in turn, will send one to us to keep in a sacred space. Pretty soon, we were sending each other positive prosperous texts daily, when possible.

Here are examples of messages one might send: **"I am filled with Divine Love, thus I prosper *now*"** or **"Divine Wisdom leads me to the perfect prosperous actions *now*".** Notice the word *now*. Remember to state your abundance to be specific and blessed in the present. We want to send these messages to people who are receptive and supportive. This is the act of planting Divine ideas that will manifest in time, in miracles.

Bonus days 17 - 20

You may even be fortunate enough to get a group of 2 to 4 people together weekly or monthly with the specific intent of lifting each other. This can create a lifted consciousness for everyone involved. You can even turn your exercise class into an uplifting get together. Anytime more than one is gathered with the intent of improving, there is great opportunity to lift. Remember when you uplift another you uplift yourself. Setting the intention to create an empowering space for your group shall enhance each other's lives.

Forgiveness

I now remember how truly Divine I AM and what a miracle I AM. I make the commitment to love myself more every day and I accept my true magnificence. I remember that I AM an extension of God energy; this confirms that I AM precious. My natural state is of a radiant, loving being. My heart and mind are now filled with the truth of my Holiness. I AM a sacred Treasure. I will start treating and talking to myself in a way that reflects my Divinity Now. I now remember that God, the unsurpassed supreme being of the universe created a perfect Divine being in me. I realize that I have ignored this detail for far too long and I now reclaim my inheritance as a Divine child of God. I forgive myself for any time I felt less than magnificent, perfect or Divine. I forgive myself for anything I did conscious or unconsciously in the past that hurt myself or another. I forgive anyone in my life that hurt me consciously or unconsciously. I choose to set myself free with the Divine power of forgiveness. I finally see the perfection of everything through God's eyes and I AM Grateful! Thank you, my Lord for this remarkable being that I AM. I feel your love and it lifts me. I feel your pride in me and I AM renewed and content again. My dear Lord, in all your brilliance, you created me and I AM a miracle.

Day 21

WRITING OUT A NEW PRODUCTIVE SCRIPT

"Imagination is more important than knowledge."

---Albert Einstein

Telling the story the way we want things to be during "challenging" times takes practice, but we can wake up and do this. **This is an important part of our work. As we are clearing out old unproductive programs and emotions, we need to write out a new script. Write out our lives the way we want them to be.** When we are dealing with a situation that we are not happy with, it is up to us to stop, become conscious, and use one of our powerful clearing tools. Make a practice of seeing yourself in a better place. Understand that as we relax and allow our Divine mind to flow, the perfect solutions will come to us and things do shift for the better. It is also important to make peace with where we are. As we release the old unproductive programming from our past, we make room for a beautiful new story to develop and take root.

Try smiling and taking your mind to a better place; this is our work. Look for a story that makes you feel blissful. The only

DAY 21

way to know this works is to try it. Stop telling the negative story right now and tell a positive one. If fear has taken over, which is natural at times, use some of the tools in this book like writing it out and ripping up the paper, knowing the situation is lifting for the better. Use the Switchword, "Bluff," which is to release fear. Simply say, "bluff, bluff, bluff," and turn your attention to something you like. Once while visiting a friend in the hospital. He said "I feel like I am trapped in this hospital." I reminded him that his mind can go anywhere he likes. I personally take my mind to my favorite places every time I catch myself thinking fearful thoughts. This is one of my favorite tools right now. I take a friend to a beautiful beach where we laugh and play anytime I like. This raises my vibration and puts me in a great mood regardless of where I am or what is going on around me. I love to do this when someone is talking about negative things. I simply go to my "happy place" in my mind and stare with my little secret smile.

Let me get you started with some general statements that you can apply to many aspects of your life. Let's talk our way up to a better feeling place. Feel free to create your own. Here we go:

"Things seem a little rough right now, but they always get better for me. I will breathe and center myself."

"Divine Wisdom is flowing through me now, giving me the perfect solution."

"I am a really good person and I am doing the best I can."

DAY 21

"The other people in this situation are really doing the best they can."

"We just let a little fear get the best of us, but we are seeing things more clearly now and have a whole new perspective that will serve us."

"Things are really not that bad. I really have a pretty good life."

"I am feeling a little better every minute."

"I can do this; I actually have many blessings in my life.I will write my blessings down now."

"Ah, that feels better; everything is going to be fine."

Do you see how much better that train of thought felt? That is one example. You will want to play with it and find your own soothing words. There will be times when it takes longer to release our negative emotion. Just keep at it and be patient. Things will shift for the better.

Work with the Divine tools in this book and set the intention to release stuck negative emotion and old unproductive programs. Have faith that God and your angels are on the job and will help you to align things at the perfect time. Meditation is a very important part of helping us stay in a good place mentally more often. As we meditate regularly, we will connect with Divine Energy and, with practice, quiet raging thoughts. We develop the ability to bring this calm into the rest of our life. It takes

Day 21

determination and consistency, but it is well worth the effort. You will learn that you can return to this quiet place in your mind when the stresses and problems of the day try to take over. Once we step back, take a deep breath and connect to our Divine wisdom, we will remember that all things are possible when we quiet the mind and see things through Divine eyes. Telling a better story is a wonderful practice to start now.

Day **22**

SETTING DIVINE INTENTION

*"Once you make a decision,
the universe conspires to make it happen."*

---Ralph Waldo Emerson

Once we become conscious of our power to create more of the life we desire, it is a very good idea to take time each day to set our Divine Intentions. It always amazes me how once we "set our minds to what we want," things start moving. It is as if Heaven and Earth start to accommodate us in our desires once they are discovered and focused upon. Setting Divine Intentions is very easy; simply make some decrees of what you would like in your life.

Let's make some now. Feel free to use these or create your own. If you want to give them some more power, write them down and keep them in a special place. The Red Envelope Technique in this book is a version of this.

Here are some examples of decrees:

"It is my Divine Intention to flow through the day with more peace, love and joy in my heart."

Day 22

"It is my Divine Intention to keep my mind open to the God within me. I now remember that everything is always working out for the best and I can relax and enjoy my life now.*"*

"It is my Divine Intention to allow God's Love to flow and direct every relationship in my life. When I get angry or hurt by someone, I intend to become conscious and know that we are all doing the best we can in every moment. I will respond with love now. *"*

"It is my Divine Intention to find a path in life that brings me great joy while helping others and prospering. I am open to allowing miracles now. *"*

"It is my Divine Intention to always remember that God is the source of my supply and relax in the knowledge that I will always have everything I need at the perfect time."

"It is my Divine Intention to remember that when I experience challenges in life, I will always be given the strength I need at the time."

As we start to set Divine intentions, they will become more familiar to us. When negative thoughts intrude, this practice will pay off as we replace the fearful thought with a Divine intention.

Day 23

APPRECIATING MISTAKES

"There are no mistakes, no coincidences. All events are blessings given to us to learn from."

---Elizabeth Kubler-Ross

When we get in a place of expecting ourselves and others to be perfect, this is unrealistic. We will all make mistakes. There are going to be times when we get upset and out of our alignment. Even the most successful and spiritual people have off days. When we do get upset or make mistakes, it is infinitely more productive to be easy on ourselves about this. I believe that getting upset also "clears the air" and creates room for better things to come.

It is important to understand that we always learn so much from our mistakes and challenges. Thomas Edison was asked by a young reporter if he felt like a failure and thought he should give up on trying to invent the light bulb. Edison replied "Young man, why should I feel like a failure? And why would I ever give up? I now know over 9000 ways the electric light bulb will not work. Success is almost in my grasp." Shortly after over 10,000 attempts, Edison invented the light bulb.

DAY 23

Once we admit our mistake, we can start learning and getting our lessons from it. If we try to blame others, then we lose the many benefits. Smart people admit their mistakes easily and know they will learn from them. We are taught in school and jobs that mistakes are bad. This is why some people just give up. What we need to understand is that the more challenging a goal is, the more setbacks we are likely to encounter and learn from them.

I love what the beautiful Sophia Loren said: "Mistakes are part of the dues one pays for a full life." I encourage you to see the beauty in your mistakes and call them good in order to move on. We want to embrace our mistakes and challenges, understanding that the only mistake is being afraid to make one.

Day 24

DIVINE LOVE OF SELF

"Do you want to meet the love of your life? Look in the mirror."

---Byron Katie

My favorite line from *The God Memorandum* by Og
Mandino is, "You are God's Greatest Miracle." During challenging
times, this reminder has lifted me. Deep self love is key to a
fulfilling life. This is because we must first love and appreciate
ourselves in order to ever receive it from others. It is human nature
to want to fill ourselves up and get our self-esteem from others.
**This is a dangerous trap as people are fickle and may love us
one moment and not the next. Depending on others to make us
feel good can leave us starving emotionally. We have all looked
to others to do this for us, but feeling good has and always will
be an inside job.** When we feel like people are taking too much
and not giving us anything in return, this is the perfect time to
write it all out on paper until it feels better. Maybe they are and
maybe they are not. This is not about blame but about taking
personal responsibility so we may go to our vast never-ending
source so we may fill back up. Realizing that no human can do this
for us is empowering. Many times we are expecting Divine acts

DAY 24

from simple humans. It is just not fair to them or us. Look to yourself and God.

We must also understand that it is not our responsibility to make anyone else happy. One of my favorite Abraham-Hicks messages is you cannot stand on your head enough ways to make everyone else happy. Once we please one, there will always be another to please. Anytime we find ourselves upset by the actions of others, this is great time to write out all the hurt and anger we feel in order to release it. After we get out what is bothering us, we may fill back up with more of what we want. Here are some positive loving decrees to practice:

"Everything I need is within me. I take deep breaths and fill with Divine Love now."

"I am blessed and abundant by nature. Everything comes to me at the perfect time in the perfect way."

"Together with Divine Wisdom, I am seeing the perfect path for all things wanted to magnetize to me now."

"I am blessed with the ability to see the light in others easily."

And one of my favorites: "What others think of me is none of my business."

Make these Divine decrees to yourself often until self love becomes a habit.

DAY 24

It is a blessed individual who understands the brilliance of coming from our power. As we come to understand this, we surely do set a beautiful example for those around us. There is no one more important we give appreciation and love to than ourselves. God worships and adores us; when we understand this and start emulating God, we are on our way. People around us will magically become more loving or disappear to make room for people who really feel this way. **Never look back and waste time wondering why a certain person was not kind to you; simply start being kind and loving to yourself.** This is something that we shall want to consistently work on. Take time in your day to do nice things for you and talk lovingly to yourself; the payoffs are big. Stop looking to anyone else to make you feel good.

Look to God and yourself now to fill up with Divine Love. Sing to yourself, buy yourself beautiful flowers, smile, take time for the things you love, take hot relaxing baths with candles and special soothing salts, meditate, play your favorite sport regularly, take up that hobby you always wanted to, actively look for joy, do those things you want others to do for you for yourself now and watch yourself blossom. This takes a lot of determination. We will all have moments when we are better at this than others, but we have a goal of self love and this is a beautiful thing.

You will also fill up and get great self esteem by doing selfless acts for others. It is amazing how when we take the focus off ourselves and help another, things shift beautifully for the better. One of my favorite examples of this is a wealthy man who

Day 24

was experiencing health challenges. He had been to all the best doctors and tried everything. He was in a yoga class and inspired to ask the instructor if she had any suggestions. She told him to do selfless acts for charity. He was skeptical but just desperate enough to give it a try. The man did not return to yoga class for a month. When he finally showed up at class he was thrilled to report that since becoming involved in a charity that helps others, his own health concerns had taken a "back burner" and were clearing up a little more each day. This goes to the knowing that when we help another, we help ourselves. It really is that simple.

We prosper from our strong knowing that we are our own best friend and deserve to feel the love that we and God can provide. How exciting to know that when we come from a place of strong self love, everything is working out for the best. This may include better health, Divine relationships and more of the abundance we seek. This is our birthright. Coming from self-love is the perfect place to create more of what we want. Practice often and watch your life thrive from this intelligent knowing.

THE BEAUTY OF NOW

"Look lovingly upon the present, for it holds the only things that are forever true."

---A Course In Miracles

Many masters have taught a common lesson in one form or another, including "Be here *now*," and "*Now* is where all our power is." Eckhart Tolle brought this understanding to the front of our consciousness in his inspiring book, *The Power Of Now*. Tolle beautifully explains that when we think about the past or future in a fearful way, this is a negative thought form. These thought forms are, of course, not real. We spend way too much time in fear when we are unconscious. Much of the time, we imagine the past and present as stressful, visualizing all the problems of the past and the scary things that "could" happen to us in the future. Tolle calls this problematic thinking. The cure is to become conscious of this behavior and decide that it no longer serves us, consciously grounding ourselves in our perfect now. It is becoming quite clear that all our power lies in the now and enjoying this moment.

Take the moment you are in and look around now. What is it that pleases your eyes? Look for beautiful colors. Is there someone or something in your environment right now you really enjoy looking at? Savor this moment. Take some deep breaths and just feel. Is the air cool or warm on your skin? Now smile. How

Bonus days 21 - 24

does that feel? Do you feel your power? It is always the simple things that yield powerful results. It is all in this moment. Feel the divinity of this precious moment. Remind yourself that everything is fine; you are safe and you can relax. Being in the moment is a delicious sensuous experience if we only allow it. If your mind wanders, this is fine; remind yourself in a soothing way to get back into this moment as often as possible.

When you find yourself mentally going to concerns in the past or future, try to become conscious as quickly as possible and gently remind yourself to return to the moment. Say, "I return to this perfect moment," as often as necessary. Cultivate this habit throughout your *Activate Your Abundance* program. Any new habit takes at least 21 days to start becoming part of your subconscious. As we keep ourselves in the moment, we will start to notice a peace and more space between our thoughts. This can only be understood by experiencing it, but the best way to describe it is as a sigh. The feeling of a calm mind is true joy. Then, after time we will notice that when those empty spaces are filled, it is with more uplifting thoughts.

It is also very interesting to note how often our ego tries to pull us out of the moment we are in. As we become more conscious, we become aware of the grasping nature of the mind; many times the mind wants to be somewhere else, like something so special is going on and we are missing it. As we get conscious and start soothing these thoughts, the real bliss and peace comes.

Bonus days 21 - 24

Think, "Ah, here I am and it is fine." We can make peace with this moment and this place and just relax to enjoy now.

Have you noticed that when we reach for a goal, all we think about is how happy we will be once we get it? A lot of time and energy is spent focusing on how much happier our lives will be once we get "there." This is a block that keeps us from enjoying all the love and abundance that surrounds us now. In Russell Simmons' books, he really writes about how it is the creative process and doing our art that makes us happy. He encourages us to take any job we are involved in and give it our all without worrying about the money, understanding the money will take care of itself. I find this perfect advice.

Russell explains how many of the artists he represents think that it is all about becoming famous and getting all the toys that come from money. They soon discover that yes, the toys are lovely, but they do not make us happy. It is and always will be the time spent creating and enjoying the process that gives us bliss and joy. To this I add to make the conscious decision to enjoy everything we do, be it raising great kids, mopping the floors or running a corporation. See every task as an opportunity to love our life and enjoy the process.

When we are small children, all we want to do is grow up; then, it is all about getting married or that perfect career; then, we cannot wait to have kids or get that vacation home; and then, we are looking forward to retiring. Next thing we know, it is all over.

Bonus days 21 - 24

Slow down! Be here in the moment, take deep calming breaths and smell the roses. As we learn to enjoy the moment, life takes on new meaning and the little things start to give us profound joy. As we stop looking to this "elusive future," we may enjoy life *now*, where we are. Everything is going on right now. Amazing creators like the Buddha and Jesus knew this. Children are masters at getting in and enjoying the moment. Now, we can too.

There will be days when we may only stop and get in the moment once or twice. This is fine! With practice and patience, we find ourselves enjoying the moment more often and reaping the rewards.

Illumination

MEDITATIONS FOR NIGHTS 25 - 28

I now remember that everything around me that is not love is simply an illusion. I choose to see the best in people. I choose to see God in everyone I meet. I choose to forgive everyone in my life. I realize that everyone is doing the best they can with the level they are conscious, in any moment. I remember that we all have the potential for Godliness or fear in any moment. I choose to see God in the trees and hear him in the breeze. I choose to take back my Divinity. I choose to know my power, my connection with Divine Intelligence, the source of all that is good and miraculous. I choose to remember that scarcity is just an illusion; that there is more than enough for everyone. I know that struggles are part of life, but when they occur, I choose to take my mind to all the abundance, prosperity and beauty that abound on our beautiful earth. I remember to be easy on myself and learn this all at my own pace, never judging myself as wrong when I become angry or upset. I remember that I AM human and give myself a lot of love and plenty of room for mistakes, calling it all good. I remember that in every struggle there is a present and a silver lining. I decide this very Divine moment to see all the blessings and good around me. I choose love as a healing salve that I want to spread across my whole world. I realize that there are reasons for everything that happens. I do not always have to understand these reasons; I only need to understand that God is Divine, all-knowing and resides in me now. There is a heavenly intelligence at the root of everything and l only need to have faith that everything will be alright. I understand that faith clears the channel for miracles to take place. My true power lies in my never-ending connection to you my God, my Love. This knowledge keeps me in a heavenly state. I love to come back to this Divine knowing as often as possible, becoming conscious of my true power. This Glorious Knowing flows through me now and I AM restored.

UNCOVERING THE ILLUSION

"To end the misery that has afflicted the human condition for thousands of years, you have to start with yourself and take responsibility for your inner state at any given moment. That means now."

---Eckhart Tolle,

A New Earth: Awakening To Your Life's Purpose

Scarcity is an illusion. These fears that plague us are like a bad dream. Eckhart Tolle explains that these negative fears are thought forms which have a life of their own and take us away from our peace. When we give these unwanted thought forms our attention, we start to believe they are true and give them our power. These thought forms include, "We are not safe in the future," "There is not enough for everyone," and "What if we get sick?" The list goes on, but you get the idea. These thought forms are filled with fear and anxiety. The cure is to simply become conscious of these unwanted thought forms, and they will start to lose their power over us. Any time we identify one of these unpleasant thought forms we take away its power by realizing that it is not real. We simply need to become conscious and become an

DAY 25

observer of these frantic thoughts. Becoming conscious in the moment frees our minds to peace.

We only have to wake up to our Divine inheritance and become aware. There is more than enough for everyone. Brilliant teachers like Catherine Ponder, Eckhart Tolle, John Randolph Price, Og Mandino and Abraham-Hicks share this knowing. The abundance or perceived lack a person is experiencing is merely a reflection of the thoughts they are entertaining. As we shift our thoughts and lift our consciousness, we gain a feeling of lightness and ease that is our natural state. John Randolph Price teaches an invaluable lesson in *The Abundance Book,* that, "no person, place or thing is our supply, connection to our God is our supply." As we come to understand that God and we are one, thus we are our own supply, we are filled with a peace that benefits us on all levels. Our remembrance of this truth and our connection to God is our supply. **Money is not our supply; it is simply a side effect of lining up with our Divine knowing and peace. Divine energy or God is our supply.**

Lifting our thoughts is central to getting the results we desire. This is a continuous job. We all have to stay conscious in the moment and be aware of what we are entertaining in our minds. The thoughts we entertain are either fear or love. As we make the conscious decision to choose love more often, we will receive peace of mind and abundance on all levels.

Day 26

BE OPEN TO RECEIVE NOW

"See your heart blossoming into a beautiful lotus flower and as you watch the lotus petals unfolding you see written on each petal I deserve, I receive, I am worthy, I am loved."

---Mirabai Devi, Samadhi Essence of the Divine

When we are experiencing challenges, at times things seem like they will never get better. This is when it is natural to go into fearful thoughts. These fearful imaginings are guidance telling us to choose a thought that feels a little better. What we need is a breakthrough! We do whatever it takes. We are human and at times fear is normal, but this is the time to remember that all we need is flowing to us in every moment; we want to become conscious. Right here and now is all we have. Lift your hand, take a deep breath and say: **"I am open to receive all the help, blessings, peace and abundance that is coming to me NOW."** Understand that all your power is in your perfect *now*. When we are always looking to tomorrow for our prosperity, then our good will always be a day ahead of us. As we start claiming and seeing now as the moment when all our good comes, then it does. Put the word NOW at the end of every positive affirmation you make. This is very effective and empowering. You will feel a positive rush as you make statements like **"*I AM* blessed and abundant in all**

DAY 26

things NOW" or "*I AM* filled with Divine Wisdom NOW. *I AM* in the flow NOW." These empowering affirmations are brought into the present and therefore more effective. Our subconscious really hears this and responds with secure feelings, which bring in more wonderful experiences. Be patient and have faith. Releasing old stale programming combined with positive affirmations will open us to an abundant mindset now.

KEEP NEW IDEAS TO YOURSELF

*"If you create a scene which implies the fulfillment of your desire
and dwell in it until you have an inner conviction that it is real,
what does it matter what another thinks?"*

---*Neville Goddard*

When we first conceive of a great new idea, it is just a
seedling and needs time to grow and develop strong roots. We are
full of excitement and it is normal to want to share it with others.
Here is the kicker: others might start giving us negative feedback
and this could dampen all our enthusiasm. Many times people do
not mean to be negative; it is human nature to get stuck in fear at
times and pass this on. Now, if we know someone is good at giving
positive feedback, then we may want to share a vague picture of
what we are doing with our creative ideas.

I only share my "new baby" ideas with people who I know
want me to succeed and have an uplifting attitude. I keep these
visions to myself in a very safe, nurturing environment. This is
what I call nurturing my sacred visions. Another choice is to share
these wonderful new ideas with our journal. Write down all the
great things that we are going to create and then see them clearly in
our mind. This will fuel our goals while enhancing everything with

DAY 27

the power of the written word; helping our plans come to fruition. Share these ideas with God, knowing your plans are supported.

UNDERSTANDING AND RELEASING
HOT SPOTS

*"I have decided to stick with love. Hate is too great a burden to
bear."*

---*Martin Luther King*

Natalie Hill gave me some great advice during an EFT
session. She explained that it is very beneficial to really pay
attention when something gets us upset or angry. This is our
subconscious trying to point us to an issue that needs to be cleared
for a healthier mind and body. When I began practicing this, it all
started coming together.

Here is an example of how this works: Let's say a family
member makes a passing comment, "I see where you have an
overdue bill charge." All of the sudden, we get very tense and
agitated, angry with the company who sent the overdue bill charge
and very angry with the person who told us. We feel reactive and
overwhelmed thinking all sorts of negative thoughts. This is the
time to become conscious and start tapping. As we tap on this
frustration, it would lead us to a "core" deeper issue that needs

DAY 28

clearing. For example, the issue "There is just never enough money" or "People treat me bad" is at the root of this frustration.

Over time, as we use EFT and tap on these core self-defeating issues, they are going to shift. We are no longer as reactive to these issues because of releasing the "hot spot". **Setting the intention to clear these deep issues will help to create a life of peace. Without these heavy negative thoughts in our minds, there is room for abundant thinking to take root and bloom. It will also keep us from attracting more similar unwanted things. The "hotspot" attracts unwanted things, so it is to our advantage to release it.** Understanding and working on this makes us master creators. We are really taking responsibility and will reap the rewards.

Start really paying attention when you get upset. Bless the person who upset you. They are doing you a favor by helping you to discover what needs cleaning up. It is fascinating to discover issues that have been trapped in our bodies for years and even more exciting to watch them go. You know this is working when the next time someone mentions something along the same lines that upset you before, there is not as much of an emotional charge attached to it. You may not like it, but now you can see the "hot spot" and can soothe and clear it.

RELEASING LIMITING PROGRAMS

"The mind is everything; what you think, you become."

---Buddha

Once we start to take personal responsibility and learn to heal ourselves, one of our jobs becomes paying attention and becoming aware of our self-defeating programs that are creating unwanted things. These programs stem from childhood and past hurts and are created throughout our lives. The good news is that once we become aware of them, we can start to do the real work of healing and clearing them. There is a hugely satisfying feeling that comes from understanding the origins of a negative behavior pattern or situation, realizing we can clear it for a better life. Taking responsibility puts us in our power.

Since our minds are creating and responding to these programs, it pays to release negative ones. Much of this understanding came to me through Suzanna Kennedy in her groundbreaking book, *Sacred Union*. Blair Billings, a national director for a large company, also teaches many of her 8000 consultants that it really is about becoming aware and releasing these personal limiting programs in order to have the success we desire. We all have negative experiences from our childhood and recent times that upset us. These traumas may become locked in

Bonus days 25 - 28

our mind and body, attracting more unwanted experiences like them to us.

Everyone is unique, but many people keep these disappointments locked in their subconscious and body. These are like old computer programs that play over and over, creating unwanted emotions and experiences for us. It is time to "delete" these programs. Releasing these negative programs is so freeing and empowering. We do not need to go looking for old limiting beliefs or problems, but if we catch ourselves having challenges in certain areas of our lives, it is time to take a look at what needs cleaning up and releasing.

I, personally, discovered that I had a tendency to look for things I did not like about people and find fault. I realized this was creating unhealthy patterns in my relationships. I went looking for how this got started and realized that I had been "picked on" a lot as a child. I am sure many of us have this program running. Once I got this realization, I could use my tools to clear on this self-defeating program. This pattern pops up less and less for me now. When it does, I can see it for what it is and clear on it with love. When the desire to find fault with someone comes, I start one of my clearing techniques and remind myself that everything is all right. I can take deep breaths and center myself in the now. Also now, when I find others "picking on me," I can see the pattern for what it is and not get sucked into "the drama." I can send the person love and move on to more productive things. That is the beauty of seeing these programs for what they are. This allows us

Bonus days 25 - 28

to become an "outside observer" and stay in a better place emotionally. For instance, if someone does "pick on me," it will not have as much of an emotional charge or upset me if I am conscious of this program. We can see things with clear eyes and accept people the way they are more often. This makes for much more loving relationships.

Another example would be if a person gets an ugly divorce and carries a lot of pain and anger. A program could develop that says they are an "abandoned victim." These heavy feelings are creating unwanted things; clearing them will allow for new and productive energies. The "hurt" person may find him/herself speaking and thinking negatively of their ex-spouse without even being aware of the damage it is creating. The program "I have been abandoned" may develop. This would keep potential wonderful mates and loving experiences away. They may even find themselves marrying the same type of person they wanted to get away from. This is when it will serve a person to become conscious of the lessons and gifts the situation brought them, then clear the negative emotions and program. It is so life giving to understand that as they love and appreciate their past spouse for what they brought to their life, they will be opening themselves up to a much deeper level of love and happiness. I meet people who are angry and frightened, and I just want to fill them with love and understanding. This is, of course, an inside job. We create so many blocks to love we are not even aware of. It is so empowering to ask to be shown these blocks so we may clear on them. Only the "hurt" person may become conscious and clear the negative program for him/herself. Anger has its place and needs to run its course, but once a person is ready, the healing may begin and bring a feeling of relief and joy. Holding onto blame will keep a person in victimhood and attached to dark angry emotions. Appreciating the lessons we experienced and the love we do have will create untold miracles. I would also like to add that if you are unhappy with your current mate, your best course of action is to clean things up where you are before you start looking for a new one. If we do not clean things up, we will only attract more of the same problems.

Taking full responsibility for every relationship in our lives is a wonderful place to start. This task may seem overwhelming, but if we ask Divine energy for help, we may have faith that the help we need will come at the prefect time.

Another example would be of a person who is very unhappy with their job and quits, only to find him/herself in another job that they do not like. They would want to discover the negative programs they have about work in order to attract a more fulfilling career. They may have watched their parents in an unhappy work situation and developed the program that "jobs are just hard work." Each person will need to look for their unique program -- no two programs are exactly alike. These negative programs are bringing the same unwanted situations and need to be cleaned up so we can move forward. We all have them, as we are human and this is part of the journey. The best course of action is to start cleaning and clearing on the negative programming and do everything we can to get happy where we are. We will want to

Bonus days 25 - 28

clean up everything around us in order to experience Divine states of mind and life. Running from these problems will never work as we take ourselves everywhere we go. Self-love and understanding are the way to work through them. We *deserve* to feel good -- we are so worth the effort!

Here is a list of common negative programs running that you may want to clear. These may or may not be yours; yours may be variations of these themes. Look deep and find the ones you need to clear and work on them. Even the most successful people have programs they can clear to feel better. This is not about admitting something is wrong with us. This is about taking back our power.

1. People do not like me. People are mean to me.

2. I am overweight and unattractive. I will never lose weight. I gain weight easily.

3. I have no idea how to make money. I am never going to have enough money. I will never be successful.

4. I am a bad parent. My teenager does not respect me. My children should treat me better.

5. I am not healthy. I can't enjoy healthy foods. I do not like to exercise.

6. My parents passed me bad habits. It is my parents' fault.

7. My mate does not respect me. My mate does not enjoy me or want to spend time with me.

8. I never have enough time.

9. I can't learn new things.

10. I am not safe. The world is not a safe place.

As you can imagine, if any of these programs are running, they are creating things we really do not want. Allowing these programs to stay buried will never serve us. This is about *taking full responsibility*. Becoming aware of these thoughts is hard and actually hurts. This is why it is so exciting to find our EFT, Third Eye technique and other tools found in this book. We can successfully remove these old limiting programs to enjoy the life we desire and deserve.

I love what Mirabai Devi, a respected author, says. She explains that we now have the opportunity to do a lot of cleaning in our lives for one of the first times in human evolution. As we become conscious and do this work, it will benefit us in all levels of our lives. Every day we want to practice cleaning and clearing our mind, body and spirit in order to experience Divine results.

The best course of action is to simply ask God or our higher-self to help discover and clear out any old limiting programs that are not serving us. Set the intention that this release happens with ease and for our highest good. Here is a general releasing statement you may use: **"Dear God, please help me to**

Bonus days 25 - 28

remove any limiting programs with ease. Allow Divine love and wisdom to fill any empty spaces we create."

Say this for as long and as many times as inspired. Now, be open to any forms of information or help that may come your way. Belinda Womack, author of *Angels Guide*, says God and the angels work in miracles through action. They send a person, book, exercise or any number of solutions to you. Simply use your guidance system to choose the best one for you in the moment. Clearing old limiting beliefs is different for everyone; there is no right or wrong way.

We can learn to see these times as highly productive -- like cleaning our homes -- so we may enjoy them more. The payoffs are big -- we are creating a space in our consciousness for new Divine ideas to come. We simply set the intention to release these limiting programs and Divine energy will lead the way.

There are experts who say that our old negative programs are not playing a role in our lives. My question, then, is why are so many people creating things they do not want once they become aware that they play a role in the creating process? The only answer that makes sense is that sometimes we do not know we have unconscious programs creating. Words also confuse, as subconscious may mean different things to people. The bottom line is, once we clear these known or unknown "programs" from our minds and bodies, we create a space for magnificent things.

Bonus days 25 - 28

The tools presented here are deceptively easy and will clear very effectively. It is always the simple processes that yield the best results. Have an open mind and take advantage of all our tools.

Now

I *now* realize that my Divine Mind stays in this moment. I see that this moment is all I have. I choose to put my focus on the wonderful things going on around me *now*. *I AM* blessed and abundant *now*. I know that God sees everything as perfect, so I release all judgments. Everything I need is here *now*; I relish this knowing and enjoy the beauty of the moment. I enjoy how perfect this moment is *now*. I find all the delicious details in the now. I take deep breaths and realize how perfect everything is *now*. I *now* realize how blessed I am to have my eyes, ears, voice, strong heart and too many other blessings to mention. I relish in the miracle that is me. Did I ever really pay attention to how much God has given me? I *now* see all my blessings in their entire splendor. *I AM*, in this moment, taking deep breaths and reveling in the beauty that surrounds me. Have I really looked at the beauty of a magnificent sunset or tree? Have I really appreciated this ever abundant planet which God created just for me? I see it all now and I feel an awe that brings tears to my eyes and fills me with love. All this, you did for me, God. This moment, and every moment, I will try to enjoy these infinite blessings you have bestowed upon me out of your supreme love for me. I feel your bottomless love for me *now* and know who I truly am. I am your perfect creation *now*. Never has there been another me.

I am the unique image of my God, and this pleases me. All the times I was hard on myself are over. My self-condemnation is in the past as I understand who I am now. I realize that my happiness is *now*. If *I AM* always looking to tomorrow, my bounty will always be a day ahead. As I breathe deeply into the moment, I realize that I have wasted too much time looking for the goal and not enjoying the ideal journey that *I AM* on. I realize that all my God power is in the *now* and that by simply focusing on the wonder that is me and my world, I tap into an unlimited abundance and prosperous mindset. *I AM* part of God in this moment and I shall bask in this knowledge with contentment. I shall be here *now* and look for the perfection of this moment. Thank you, God; this feels Divine.

Day 29

FOCUS

"As you become definite about prosperity, it becomes definite about you. As you turn the great energy of your thinking upon ideas of plenty, you will have plenty, regardless of what people about you are saying or doing."

---Catherine Ponder

There is a universal law that states what we focus on we get more of in our life. Now that we are aware of this law, we are going to get very specific about exactly what we focus on. We are sending a strong message out when we know what we want and ask for help from God, Divine Energy. This works and has a universal law behind it. Call in your childlike qualities. Here are some ideas to play with -- you may even get creative and enhance them with your own flavor! Have an open mind with these techniques and enjoy the process.

On checks you send, in the memo spot at the bottom left of the check, write initials to state the abundance you are attracting. Here are some examples: write "IAMA," which stands for "*I AM* Abundant" or "IAMBN," which stands for "*I Am* Blessed Now." This reminds you of your blessings and sends out a strong message to create more of what you want. On deposit slips to your banking

DAY 29

account, write the initials "TMTC," which stands for "There's More to Come," to remind yourself that your supply is never ending and flowing. These are simple techniques that create powerful results.

This focuses our mind; the more we practice this with intention, the more prosperous we will feel. The more prosperous we feel, the more prosperous we will become. Neville Goddard, an amazing prosperity teacher, stated, "Whenever your feeling is in conflict with your wish, feeling will be the victor."

If you feel a little silly doing this, just keep it to yourself. No one has to know what you are doing but you. This way you will keep the energy strong and in a positive place. Never tell anyone anything you are doing unless you know they will give you a positive response. Keep your dreams to yourself until they come into being and you are feeling confident.

Here is an abundance card to copy and keep in your wallet, where you can see it easily.

Abundance and Love

flow easily into my life

DAY 29

This card will remind us of just how prosperous we are every time we spend or put money in our wallet. Activate this card by setting the intention that you align with more of what you want. The sideways 8 on the card is the sign of infinity, signifying a never-ending supply of all you could ever want or need.

I give these cards to anyone I feel is receptive and I have gotten some great success stories. One of my friends said that right after she activated and put the card in her wallet, she received a hundred dollars "out of the blue."

Fold your money with the intention of "making more." Stack your bills with the largest to smallest in order. For instance put your twenties first, next your ten dollar bills, now your fives and your ones all in order. Now fold them, with the ones on the outside and say to yourself "make more." This sets the intention and sends a strong message to the universe. How does your wallet look? Is it crammed with unnecessary papers and junk? Clear it out and create a space for more abundance to flow.

If these ideas feel a little "childish," remember children are wonderful creators; we can learn so much from them. An open mind will serve us well.

Day 30

SCREEN THE MEDIA YOU WATCH

"Be gentle with yourself. You are a child of the universe, no less than the trees and the stars. In the noisy confusion of life, keep peace in your soul."

---Max Ehrmann

Now that we understand the power of feeling good, it is time to become very picky about what we watch or read. The media has a tendency to focus on the negative things taking place in the world. It is really a misrepresentation; there are so many great things going on all the time. Does it really do anyone any good to focus on the negative?

Simply decide that feeling good is a priority and look for things that lift you when you watch TV, or turn it off. TV and media, like anything else, can be used positively or negatively. If we consciously make the decision to look for uplifting programs, we will find them. This means you need to turn off any negative news. Many people may say that we need to be informed and that we are "sticking our heads in the sand" by choosing not to watch negative news. May I respectfully say that a balance is required? If you need to watch the news, just be sure to limit your time and pay

DAY 30

attention to how it makes you feel. You may find that "less is more" when it comes to the media. **As you come to understand the law that states you get more of what you focus on, you will want to start focusing on things that make you happy.** These are love, vibrant well-being and prosperity, to name a few. For those that say this law cannot be seen and therefore does not exist, I remind them that we cannot see gravity, but it is still working.

Take the opportunity to watch shows and read books that lift you. Time spent feeling good is the best possible use of our day.

Day 31

DEEP SELF LOVE CREATES MIRACLES

"Realize you are greater than you ever considered yourself to be."

---Norman Vincent Peale

Whenever we are experiencing lack of any kind, on any level, it is time to do clearing and an "intensive self love treatment." Sounds advanced, right? An intensive self-love treatment is simply telling yourself over and over how wonderful you are and how much you love and appreciate yourself. Remember that your creator is a genius and only creates Divine beings. Call on the Angels and God to fill you with Divine Love. This can be done anytime and anywhere. You will be amazed by the incredible peace you obtain by doing this. Belinda Womack wrote a lovely book called *Angel's Guide*, which is filled with the message of how much the Angels and God love us and are always here for us. This is a comforting and empowering message that we need to take deep into our conscious daily.

Louise Hay gives us a simple tool in her book *You Can Heal Your Life*. She suggests we simply say "I approve of myself" over and over. This lifts our self-esteem on a deep level.

DAY 31

Whenever I feel my mood sinking and remember to do this, I always feel a lift. It just feels reassuring to say and feel approval and self love.

As we remember to love ourselves, we become the bright, beautiful person we really are. This attracts others to us who see this and appreciate us more than we ever imagined people would.

Here is an example of how to do a deep self-love treatment and when it should be used. Let us say, for instance, that we are not happy about the fact that a person spoke rudely to us. First, use our tapping or any releasing technique to ease the negative feeling and soothe ourselves so we can move to higher thoughts. It is natural to be angry, so clear on this so we can send some love and get centered in the now. Here is an example of what we could say to ourselves after our tapping calms us:

"I now choose to become conscious and be in the moment."

" I realize that this negative emotion is not serving me."

"Wow, I am really doing the best I can."

"Maybe I misunderstood this person's reaction. They are clearly having an off day and it really has nothing to do with me."

"I am so smart to figure this out."

"I am really quite good at what I do and everyone here is lucky to have me around."

DAY 31

"I really like how good I feel as I talk myself into a better place."

"I am coming back in my power now."

      You get the picture. It feels wonderful to stay conscious enough to talk up to yourself regardless of what others are doing around you. **Remember that we cannot control the actions of others, only our response to them. This is how we stay in our power and allow more of what we want.**

MUSIC'S DIVINE NATURE

"Music washes away from the soul the dust of everyday life."

---Berthold Auerbach

Inspiring music can automatically put us in a state of bliss and peace. When we find music that appeals to us personally, we can lift our mind and spirits to a lovely state. There is a vibrational healing taking place on deep levels, a connection to Divine forces we cannot see but feel at the core of our being.

Consciously use music for lifting and creating on new levels. As we listen to beautiful music, take note of the deep chords being struck in our being. I am always in awe of how profoundly the right music can lift and touch my inner world. Divine energy is flowing freely through, clearing all the blocks. Of course, everyone will have different music that moves him or her. Look for music that lifts and inspires you. Music is so personal. Learn to use music to bring a sense of joy and enthusiasm to your life.

When I hear one of my favorite singers Donna De Lory sing the beautiful chant Lokah Samasta Sukhino Bhavantu, which means may all beings be happy and free and may my life be a giving to this happiness and freedom for all, I get lifted to new

DAY 32

heights each time. Certain music delivers a message and vibration of peace and well-being beyond compare.

We can use music to calm us. I was sitting in the doctor's office waiting while a little procedure was being done. I was so nervous and knew that the more relaxed I became, the better things would go. I pulled out my headphones and the perfect soothing song came on.

I was quickly calmed and put in a bit of a state, as I felt the soothing sounds vibrate through my body. I felt my mind quieting as the sounds healed and regenerated me. The procedure went off perfectly and I know Divine music really helped.

Each morning I love to start my day with a beautiful walk in nature. For me, uplifting music is a must. I take deep breaths as the Divine beat helps me move with ease and joy.

I am typing this book as soothing music plays and connects me with my God source, allowing this information to flow. As the tone and beat plays, Divine ideas flow to and through me. Music has the ability to make us feel and lift that is beyond words or explanation.

Singing and humming have a very uplifting effect on the body, mind and spirit. Chanting is practiced with calming and centering effects in many religions. I was blessed to meet a yoga master who practiced chanting and yoga for decades. He explained that it is not the meaning of the words that create the benefits

DAY 32

millions of people receive from chanting daily. Actually, it is the vibration of sound in the throat. The vibration soothes and lifts the whole individual, clearing and healing our energy centers. Chanting actually heals the body on many and deep levels. In my humble opinion, singing happily has the same positive effect. Try it; sing with a light, happy heart a song you really love and experience lifted states. When practiced on a consistent basis, you can expect to feel better consistently. A perfect example of this is how children often sing happily and stay in a great place.

The applications of music to enhance our lives are endless; as we take advantage of this, we are lifted to new heights.

ACCESS ALL YOUR ANSWERS

"Your all-knowing intuitive Truth lives deep inside your thinking mind and speaks out to you constantly, no matter where you are or what you are doing."

---Belinda Womack, Angels Guide

It is important to be aware that we all have access to Divine guidance and the answers we seek. This is accessed by simply getting still and listening for that still place in all of us. A wonderful way to allow answers to flow is to simply ask, be patient and wait. Have faith they will come. I am always amazed at the different ways the Divine will speak to me. It may come from a deep knowing, another person, a book, a song or other source. Years ago I went to a workshop where Abraham-Hicks spoke. I was experiencing a lot of headaches. I kept raising my hand. I was desperate to be called on so I could get some advice. I was never called on and finally just gave up. During the lunch break my husband and I sat with a couple. We all enjoyed each other's company and at the end of lunch, "out of the blue" the girl mentioned that she had been called on at her last Abraham seminar to get her question answered. I casually asked what her question was. Tears came to my eyes when she said she had gotten help with headaches. I knew God was talking to me through this woman. She explained that the most important thing to do was

Bonus days 29 - 32

relax and not worry so much about the headaches. She explained that worrying was actually making them worse and last longer. I slowly learned to just relax and the problem disappeared over time.

It is said that most of man's problems stem from the inability to sit quietly alone in a room for periods of time. There are times when things seem hopeless or we feel overwhelmed. My grandfather always said, "When you do not know what to do; do nothing." This is sage advice. During this period of getting very still or simply relaxing and taking our mind to what we appreciate, we will be lining up with wonderful solutions.

Tranquility

I quiet my mind now to hear the Lord. I know now that I need to listen for God's Divine Wisdom that flows through me all the time. I have been too consumed with my fear to listen for Him. The negative thoughts in my mind have spread like weeds, but no more. I now tend to my mind's garden with love and care. I remember that God is constantly guiding me. I now open my mind, heart and inner ears to hear God's Guidance. I now feel His direction in every cell in my body. My body, mind and spirit are filled with God and His support. God has always been speaking to me, but many times I was not still and quiet enough to hear, consumed with fear.   Now I AM. God's Divine message that I AM love and His finest creation fills me with glee. God is my rock and is always there when I need Him; I AM never alone. I AM now open to receive. I enjoy knowing that God made the sun, moon and stars just for me. I know that God's love for me has never wavered, no matter what I may have done. I feel the depth of God's love and the adoration He feels for me. This gives me a new strength and I am becoming renewed. Every day I AM filled with God's voice as the birds sing and the sun rises. I remember God did this all for me and I AM whole. I AM complete with Divine Wisdom. My cup is filled and I shine this light on the world. As I take in this Divine Nourishment, I AM born again to the new me. I AM becoming complete in this moment.

THE PROSPEROUS PRACTICE OF SPACE CLEARING

*"Empty out old dead thoughts and be reborn in mind and spirit.
That experience will make you come alive."*

---Norman Vincent Peale

I first discovered space clearing from Karen Kingston's book, *Creating Sacred Space with Feng Shui.* This fascinating practice lifts and clears the energy in our environment. For centuries, different cultures have used sound and smoke to lift and clear the energies in their environments. This is why some churches burn incense. When we clear and lift the energy in our home, it will benefit everyone who lives there.

Energy can get stagnate in corners and will freshen when it is moved out. This is why the Native American Indians had teepees. The round structure kept the energy flowing, without corners to get stuck in. No need to be concerned about your corners; we are going to learn space clearing tips to enhance your home and allow peace and prosperity. Space clearing is also very helpful when trying to sell or rent a home and for commercial

Day 33

properties. As the old stale energies are cleared, it creates an environment that attracts great things.

Here is how to do a space clearing. First, clean and vacuum all visible dirt and clutter. This first step alone is going to create a lifted feeling in your home. Now, let's really get focused for intended results.

Mentally or aloud, set the intention to bring more love, light and Divine energy into your home while releasing anything that is no longer for your highest good.

Ask that God and the Angels assist you in an effective clearing. You, of course, will call on the Divine Guidance that is best for you. You may prefer to call on your higher self if that feels better. Since it is becoming more accepted that we are the physical extension of the God energy, it is all the same thing.

It is now time to start your space clearing ceremony. Walk through each room and clap out the corners. Simply put your hands in each corner and clap until it feels clear. You may also clap your hand lightly against the corner of the wall, creating a vibration that will free any stuck energy.

Next, ring a bell throughout your space. Bells are excellent for releasing old, stale energy and enhancing the flow. This is why churches have bells. Ringing bells to enhance the energy has been used in Bali for centuries. Many types of bells are available; pick one that feels very special to you. During this whole process, say

DAY 33

prayers and hold the intention for love and joy to come into your home and life. You may use any prayers you are comfortable with or simply say, **"I now call upon Divine Love to enter my home and stay."** You may have another decree or prayer you like better. There are no rules, only that it feels wonderful when you say it.

Once you have sounded out the entire house, it is time to use your sage or incense to further clear the area. The Native American Indians used sage and it is very powerful for clearing a space. If anyone in your home has not been feeling his or her best or an argument has occurred, this is another perfect time to clear. Of course wait until they have left to do your space clearing.

Light your sage or incense and carry it around each room swiping it in drawers, cabinets and corners. Set the intention for the space while you are moving your sage around. For example, call to mind all the people you love and send them blessings. When you are clearing your abundance area, give thanks for all you have and all that is coming. When you are done, make sure you have completely extinguished the sage or incense.

When you do not have the time or desire to do a full space clearing, you may do a "quick lift" for excellent results. Take a piece of incense that you enjoy the smell of, light it and move it all through your home while setting the intention for more love and light. Say prayers or positive affirmations as you do this. This is a

DAY 33

great way to keep things fresh between full space clearings. You will be guided as to which procedure is needed by what feels good.

Once you are complete with your clearing, always wash your hands. You can expect miracles in the way of unexpected fun surprises. They can come in any size and shape, so simply be open to amazing things. Each person is unique and will experience different blessings.

Do not be alarmed if things shift or break. It is always for your highest good. Once, a few days after I had done a clearing, someone in my home "accidentally" broke our old thermostat. I was a little annoyed for a few minutes, when suddenly it dawned on me that this probably happened for a reason. I went and checked out both thermostats and sure enough, they had actual mercury in them. As you are probably aware, mercury is a toxic substance and I immediately knew I wanted it out of our home.

We had lived with these thermostats over four years and I had never even known about them as the mercury was concealed. I had both of the thermostats replaced with new digital ones, and the air and heat system now runs so much more efficiently.

You will notice that everyone in the home gets along better after you do a space clearing. I personally only space clear about every one to two months. Of course, that may vary. When you first start doing space clearings, more may be required. Once your home feels right, you can just do touch-ups to keep things light and

DAY 33

bright. After you try space clearing and notice how good it feels, you will know when one needs to be done by instinct.

If you are selling or trying to rent a home, space clearing is invaluable. I had an acquaintance that had rental property. They had some bad luck with getting good tenants. After a tenant with many problems decided to move out, I explained the benefits of space clearing and helped her do one. Within two weeks, she got a wonderful new tenant that has been a pleasure to work with.

Other things you may experience after space clearings are enhanced relationships, unexpected checks, projects moving forward, people giving you beautiful things and many other pleasant surprises. You will love the way your home feels after you take control and space clear with the intention of bringing in Divine Love.

DIVINE LEVERAGE

*"Action that is inspired from aligned thought is joyful action.
Action that is offered from a place of contradicted thought is hard
work that is not satisfying and does not yield good results."*

---Esther Hicks

Divine leverage is the ability to work smarter, not harder. The leverage I present here is focusing our thoughts to feel our best, understanding that this will enhance any activity we embark upon. As we start to practice feeling good before we take action, we will notice that we are more often in the right place at the right time, find more of what we are looking for and just flow through the day with a happy rhythm. We come to understand the benefits of feeling good *before* we take action, and always use this leverage to our advantage so things flow in a Divine way for us.

People who accomplish amazing things do not have anything more than you or me. They are using leverage by enjoying what they do to create more of what they want, whether they know it or not. This can be described as a passion for the creating process. We have the same access to greatness as anyone we have ever admired and can accomplish wonderful things.

DAY 34

Take the saying "Do what you love and you will never work a day in your life." This goes to the leverage that comes from being happy. When we are enthusiastic and passionate about what we do, things flow and come to us in miraculous ways. Look for things you love, and more things like them will come to you. What do you love doing? How can you serve others in a capacity that gives you joy? I heard a saying once that explains this, "to serve is to rule." When we help others from a place of love, we lift ourselves and benefit everyone involved.

Taking action without getting centered mentally equals a waste of time. So, next time you are about to take action, stop and ask yourself, "How does this feel? Am I in a good place mentally and in my power? Or, do I need to take a moment and step back from this situation to align my thoughts to allow peace and brilliance?"

If we are feeling frustrated or that things are not going our way, this is the perfect time to take some deep breaths and a meditation break if possible. When we are experiencing continued negative thoughts, becoming conscious of this is the first step. The next step is to quiet the mind with meditation. Quieting the mind allows Divine Wisdom to come in and adjust our perspective and emotions. Deep breathing also pulls in God energy and clears our channel for clearer communication. In case you are not in a convenient place or do not have time to meditate, make the most of your circumstances by asking God and the angels for help. Here is a decree: **"Dear God and my angels, please help me connect**

DAY 34

with my Divine self now; help me remember that everything is in perfect order. I wish to remember that things are working out for the best and I can relax now."

It is said that:

$$
\begin{array}{c}
\text{deep breathing} \\
\underline{+ \text{ positive thoughts}} \\
= \text{enhanced ability to manifest great things}
\end{array}
$$

Turn your exercise class into an uplifting experience by making positive affirmations with every lift and move. Turn off the TV and pick up an inspirational book and underline your favorite parts. This will start us off with a wonderful mindset that will have a fantastic effect on our day and the rest of our lives.

Completing a daily 10-minute meditation session works wonders for aligning our minds with peace and love. Add the *Activate Your Abundance* meditations for maximum results. Take the time to boost your mind by getting quiet with your God-self on a regular basis. Miracles just become a part of your everyday life. As we become aware of the connection between feeling good and things going our way, we shall want to take the time to get in a lifted mindset before we go out into the world or try to accomplish anything. We want to feel great before we make phone calls or communicate with others. We want to feel good before we take action in order to get the most out of everything we do. Watch a

DAY 34

child playing; they are completely focused and enjoying life in the moment. This is true leverage.

It always amazes me how Divine energy will work its miracles and the perfect circumstances will present themselves at the perfect time. For instance, I had been stuck in negative emotion for a day, which is far more than I like to tolerate. I kept praying and asking for relief. The next morning, I had to take my dog for a walk even though I wanted to hide my head under the covers.

I put on my audio player, not knowing what it would play. I was pleasantly surprised to hear one of my favorite motivational authors, Catherine Ponder, speaking about the power of focusing on what we want. As I listened to Ponder's enthusiasm and knowing, I felt myself being gently lifted back up to feeling good and I knew that everything would be alright. I have hundreds of positive audios, but I was led to the perfect one at the perfect moment. Tears came to my eyes as I was lifted back up to who I truly am and felt the Divine Love that resides in all of us. This was no coincidence, there are no accidents; Divine Wisdom is always working its magic. I love what Albert Einstein said, "There are two ways to live your life… One is as though nothing is a miracle; the other is as though everything is a miracle." I choose to see the second.

Do not worry that you do not feel good all the time; we are human and this is part of life. Ask God and your Angels for help and just allow yourself to be where you are, knowing that the

DAY 34

heavy thoughts will pass. It is proven that we can only hold a thought for so long and then it changes. Be patient and have faith while looking for things to make you feel good now. Something will come along to distract us from our "bad mood" like a great song, uplifting CD, book or conversation with a friend to lift us at the perfect moment.

I love what Abraham-Hicks discussed on one of their monthly CDs. They explained that the best part of feeling good is when we first move into that joyful feeling when we first swing into that moment of knowing life is wonderful and we are invincible. They explained that after a while, we find something to pull ourselves out of that contented feeling place but there is no need to worry. We know we can return to feeling better when we want. Any time we are not feeling our best mentally, we may remind ourselves that when we finally allow ourselves to move into joy, it will be worth the wait. It is a comforting feeling to know that good moods are always waiting for us; we have only to allow them. One of the most helpful things we can do is simply to allow ourselves to be where we are. Allow the bad mood to occur and understand that it will lift at the perfect moment. The less we push against any negative emotion, the quicker it will shift to something better. I know when we are stuck in negative emotion it feels like it will never end, but have faith and know Divine help is on its way.

Day 35

DIVINE TIMING

"Always bear in mind that your own resolution to succeed is more important than any one thing."

---Abraham Lincoln

We have all heard the saying, "Timing is everything." As we come to understand how many benevolent forces are working for us, it becomes obvious that we do not need to rush anything. Everything comes at the perfect time when we allow it.

You will discover that when things are not moving as quickly as you would like, there is actually a missing step that will make things much better once we allow it. The more patient we are, the better things turn out. When we just relax and let go, things get easy and flow in a balanced rhythm. We also find that as we give our projects or relationships the time they need, they just sort themselves out in a perfect way -- Divine Order, if you will. Be patient and feel free to use these decrees: "Divine timing is the order of the day," or "I allow Divine Mind to put everything in perfect order now."

When this book was supposed to be finished it became "stuck." I was frustrated, but it just would not move. That little

182

DAY 35

voice in my head kept saying "be patient," but this is easier said than done. So for over a month, nothing would move. I would ask the smart people in my life like my daughter if I should just relax, and the answer was of course everything will be fine, be patient. During this period I found many more important additions to this book and I now know that this delay was perfect and the best thing that could have happened. We benefit when we practice being patient and allowing the soup to simmer so that all the right components have time to come together. You know you are on the right path as you learn how to work with your faith and patience. This is a skill and, like anything else, takes practice.

Day 36

LIVING IN FREEDOM

"For life and death are one, even as the river and the sea are one."

---Kahlil Gibran

I hesitated tackling the subject of death, as it is so loaded with preconceptions and fear. Many of us are fearful because, quite frankly, no one really knows what happens after we die. With that said, we still need to get a proper attitude about death in order to live our lives to the fullest.

One of the wonderful gifts the Abraham-Hicks teachings have given many people is helping to dispel the fear of death and understand it a little better. When we start to realize that many of the worries we hold about death have no substance, we can live our life with more peace and freedom.

For instance, what if death, the one thing we are all going to do, is not a bad thing? And what if worrying about death is keeping us from truly living and enjoying our lives now?

The author of the timeless classic, *The Alchemist,* Paulo Coelho made a Divine comment in an interview that was very

DAY 36

soothing. He was asked if he believed in life after death. He said, "I am having a life after death experience now." This is a perfect answer because it speaks to the eternalness of our souls. It is really the "not knowing" that we are afraid of. Once we remember that everything will be all right, we can relax into our lives now.

I love to tell my children and anyone who wants to listen, "There is no death, merely a moving back into the non-physical." I know this is a lot to expect anyone to accept at first, but this knowing soothes many. What does your gut tell you? Do you feel that you have always just been? Since the purpose of this book is to empower and bring us peace, this is the thought process that will serve us best concerning death.

Just take this in at your own pace and integrate this knowledge into your being in your own time and way. It will serve you in ways you never imagined. Worrying gives us something to do but never really gets anything done and blocks a lot of our good. We are practicing a way of thinking that will keep us connected to Divine Wisdom more often.

I love this simple explanation Abraham-Hicks gives. Imagine you are in a movie theatre with a group of friends. You are watching and enjoying the movie with them. One of your friends decides to get up and leave. You do not worry as you know you will see them later. This is the way death is. We will see everyone later, so just sit back, relax and enjoy the show. Once we start to

Day 36

integrate this powerful knowing into our being, we can enjoy life on a whole new level.

Think about it; maybe there is nothing to fear but fear itself. Of course no one knows for sure, but what does your gut tell you? When we are worrying about what a bad thing death is, this feels really painful. This is our guidance system telling us to choose another thought. When we think thoughts more in alignment with our God self, they feel much better, thoughts like "you know everybody transitions on sooner or later, so it must be a natural part of life. When we relax about this we can enjoy life even more. Knowing that one day we are going to pass can help us pay attention a little more today and enjoy our lives to the fullest."

The classic children's book, *Tuck Everlasting,* does an amazing job of explaining why death is such a necessary part of life. My daughter read this book to me and it has a beautiful message. The Tucks are a family who drink some magic water that makes them eternal. They will never age past the point where they drank the water. After time it becomes painfully obvious to this family that all the cycles of life have their purpose. That to grow up, old and transition to the next place has its value. They become weary of just existing and never aging while those around them get to experience the natural rhythms of life. People think it would be great to live forever as the same person, but the Tucks find out this is not true. This story gives death a lovely understanding and purpose.

DAY 36

There is obviously Divine Mind behind this brilliant life; let's just trust that everything is going to be alright. It just feels good to think these thoughts! We can relax now -- it really is a soothing process. Let's make up our mind that we are going to focus on the thoughts that serve us best and work on making them our own. We do this *now*.

As we stop giving our energy and life over to fear of things we cannot control, we will be enjoying life in a whole new way. We shall be determined and say, "I am going to keep my mind in a good place as often as possible," and every time we do, we get a little stronger and better at staying in our power. Of course there will be times when we will slip; be accepting and loving of yourself. We shall always find our way back to feeling good.

11 WAYS TO LIFT A DOWN MOOD UP

*"Refuse to fall down. If you cannot refuse to fall down, refuse to
stay down, lift your heart toward heaven like a hungry beggar, ask
that it be filled and it will be filled."*

---*Clarissa Pinkola Estes*

1. Accept your mood and self like you are -- remembering
   you are human. This will take the pressure off and help you
   to relax into a better place. If we resist it, this only gives it
   more power. What we resist persists. So just accept your
   mood and know it will lift at the perfect time.

2. Meditate. Take in deep breaths, remembering your
   connection to God.

3. Write it out. Write out all the hurt and anger. Vent on a
   piece of paper and when you feel relief, rip up the paper.

4. Start counting your blessings. Hold each one for as long as
   possible. Appreciation quiets the ego and allows Divine
   mind to flow.

5. Listen to some uplifting music that feels good. Music has a
   quality that can lift the mind and spirit dynamically.

Bonus days 33 - 36

6. Take a long bath or shower (water clears and lifts your energy). Add sea salt for clearing and lifting.

7. Watch a funny movie or read an uplifting book.

8. Exercise while speaking loving thoughts to yourself.

9. Do positive uplifting things for others (this really helps, by taking the focus off us and lifting another). The smallest kindnesses can make a wonderful impact.

10. Go in nature and appreciate its splendor. If possible, take your shoes off and connect with the earth. The electromagnetic fields lift and balance your mood. The earth can pull negative emotion off us and transmute it into something higher. Large bodies of water do the same. This is why so many people love to be around water; we instinctively know it lifts and heals us.

11. Get really quiet and listen for your God. The saying, "Be still and know that I AM" says it all. Ask God and your angels for guidance and help. They can only help when asked.

Prosperity

I now understand that all my prosperity and abundance begins with a lifted state of consciousness. I understand and take in the knowledge that the life I deserve begins in my Powerful Unlimited Mind. I remember that I AM Abundance. I AM a radiating center for prosperity. The only limitations I face are the ones I have placed on myself. My success is assured as I follow God's Divine plan. This plan flows easily to me as I get still and quiet. I wait on the Lord. I understand that my blessings are many and I need only look to them to expand my consciousness of all that I have. I now freely admit that I have not used my mind power to my advantage because I believed I could do it on my own and fear set in. I have accepted and allowed dark thoughts that did not serve me. I open my mind and spirit to the Divine Intelligence that has always been available to me. I release any thoughts of scarcity, lack or criticism.

I practice these lavish abundant thoughts now. When I need help, I look in nature and take pleasure in its entire splendor. The abundance in nature is never-ending and a lavish gift my God has bestowed upon me. I appreciate that God wants me to have all that He has created for me. When I am devoted and enjoying all God has given me, this feeds me to my core and endears my God to me. I understand that when I listen closely, God will lead me in the perfect direction that helps others while I enjoy what I am guided to do. I deliberately look for things to raise my mind and spirit to a

Divine Level. My consciousness is raised as I focus on the perfection that is God in me. I knowingly cultivate rich, lavish thoughts. I remember that God wants me to be prosperous and happy. I am renewed with a lifted mind now and discover my power in God, the God in me.

CREATE A SPACE FOR PROSPERITY

"Substance (gold dust, mind power) does not flow easily into a cluttered, crowded situation."

---Catherine Ponder

One of the most effective things we can do to bring more of what we want in our life is to remove anything we are not using or don't love. Clearing out clutter from our home and life creates a space to allow more of what we are wanting. This also goes hand in hand with our mental releasing of fear and negative emotions. We are clearing inside and out for a brighter more peaceful and prosperous life.

When we are having trouble aligning with what we need, it is time to release what is blocking us. If we want more love, vitality and prosperity in our life, it is very effective to clear our clutter. Something as simple as cleaning a drawer or closet can give us an overwhelming sense of accomplishment once we understand the benefits.

If we feel stuck or like we want something that will not come, this is the perfect time to clear an area. Simply throw out or give away anything you do not use or love. At first, it is a little

DAY 37

tricky to let things go. We live in a society that equates "stuff" with abundance, but if we are not enjoying or using something, it is not serving us. It is actually blocking us from things we would really love. The more unused things we release, the better we feel, and the better we feel, the more we want to clear. It is a fabulous practice. Once we start to associate releasing things with a peaceful and happy life, it will become second nature to let go of things we do not need.

We will actually start to look for things to free. The saying "less is more" explains it all.

A friend of mine mentioned she was having some financial difficulty, and I told her about the art of clearing her clutter. I suggested that she go through her abundance area and throw out or give away anything she did not use or love.

A couple of weeks later, I saw her and I asked how she was doing. She excitedly told me that after she cleared out the clutter in her abundance area, she started getting unexpected checks. She had a problem with a company not wanting to give her a refund for a trip she could not take. She said that after she cleared out her room; "out of the blue" the company just sent her a refund in the mail without her asking again.

When I discovered clutter clearing, I was very eager to give it a try. I started by clearing out a drawer. It felt so good I did another and then another. I was amazed at how easy it became, like I had been doing it all my life. Before I knew it, I was on a roll and

DAY 37

feeling wonderful. I also found pleasure in giving things away that I was not using. I love how good it makes me feel to give to others. I always seem to get something back I enjoy after I give things away. It seems too good to be true -- I give away something I do not use and something I enjoy shows up. This activity obviously creates a space for what is wanted to come.

We had a refrigerator that kept breaking down over the course of a five-year period. It was very frustrating; repairman after repairman could not fix it. After about three weeks of serious clutter clearing, I was given a brand new refrigerator. This was like a miracle. I am sure that all my clutter clearing created a space for my brand new refrigerator to come.

Once you start clearing your clutter and see how effective it is, you will never look at clutter the same way again. You now know it is blocking things you would enjoy.

Cleaning and clearing are some of my favorite tools. When I wrote the book, *How Green Smoothies Saved My Life,* I hit a period when everything just seemed stuck. All of the sudden I remembered that my upstairs room and the attic had become a storage for things we were not using since we do not go up there that often. It became so clear to me that my book needed a place to come, and I was inspired to clear all that clutter. I started removing everything that I possibly could. It felt so empowering, like I was creating the perfect space for my book to "be born into." I set the intention for my book to come easily and gave and threw away as

Day 37

much as possible. I was not at all surprised that, within days, everything started flowing perfectly again. I was guided to the perfect people and help I needed at the time.

Start by surveying your home. Is there an area that stands out as the perfect place to start clearing? If it takes a little time to decide, this is fine. Ask God and the angels for guidance. Remember: when in doubt, clear your bedroom first. Just be patient and go with the flow. No need to push; do what feels good.

Once you know which area you want to clear, get two bags, one for items you want to give to friends or charity and one bag for items that need to be thrown away. Make the commitment to fill each bag. After you have filled your bags, you are done for the day. If you feel like continuing, that is great, and if not, it will keep until your next clearing. Immediately, move anything you are going to give away to the trunk of your car or outside. This way you can see how much you have gotten accomplished and your home will feel lighter. Then, take the bag of trash to the outside garbage bin.

When I first started clearing my clutter, my family members were not that excited. I kept explaining and reinforcing that clearing our clutter was bringing us so much more of what we wanted. As time passed, it became very obvious to my family that we were becoming more happy and abundant on all levels. Now they are all very receptive to clearing our clutter and know its value.

DAY 37

I had a lovely neighbor who had tried to sell her home for almost six months. We were talking and she was telling me how frustrated she was and how badly they needed to sell their home. I explained to her how powerful clutter clearing is and that I knew it would help. She listened while I gave her all the details I have given here. Two weeks later, I was walking my dog by her home and she had a "sold" sign in her yard. I stopped to ask her if she had used the clutter clearing idea. She said, "Yes," and that she loved to clear her clutter now. She said that she had gotten rid of tons of stuff and knew this would make her upcoming move quick and easy.

Another important step is to release people or situations that do not serve us. Negative feelings and resentments toward people or situations are a block to all the good that is trying to come to us. If we feel blame or guilt toward another, this is a "hot spot" and it is time to let it go for our own good. Ask God and the angels for help in releasing these negative feelings. We can use our tapping, writing it out or any of the other tools that appeal to us.

Catherine Ponder reminds us to do general releasing statements consistently to keep our relationships and life in great shape. When we are angry or resentful toward another, even though it is our desire to get away from them, we are actually creating an invisible bond to them that is stronger than steel. Releasing them will bring us so much more peace and serenity. It serves us to release, forgive and love others as much as anything we do. It is very simple; just use a general releasing statement like:

DAY 37

"I now release this person or situation to Divine Love, knowing that only good will come from it." You may want to word yours differently; say what feels right to you. People feel your release and appreciate it on a subconscious level. If we are trying to hold onto someone who is not receptive, releasing him or her will either bring them closer or remove them from the situation so the perfect person can come. You will notice people responding to you in a more positive way when you release them.

If we are holding onto someone and expecting them to give us something we need, John Randolph Price's masterpiece, *The Abundance Book,* gives us the perfect declaration for this, **"Money is not my supply. <u>No person</u>, place or condition is my supply. My awareness, understanding, and knowledge of the all providing activity of the Divine Mind <u>within me</u>, is my supply."** To this, I say, "Amen." Let's release everyone now, knowing that Divine energy will take care of our needs so much more efficiently than any person could. When we get still and hear that Divine Guidance speaking to and through us, we are guided to the perfect action that will yield us desired results. Do not expect any person to ever come close to accomplishing the miracles God can in your life. Releasing mental and physical clutter is one of our most empowering activities. Start now.

Day 38

UNDERSTANDING THAT MONEY IS JUST ENERGY

"Abundance is not something we acquire. It is something we tune into."

---Wayne Dyer

A wealthy man once said to me, "Money is just energy, you know," like there was no doubt in his mind. When he said this, I felt the intensity of his knowing. At the time, I was young, struggling a bit and did not understand exactly what he meant. Over the years, as I started paying attention to how my attitude and thoughts affected my money or lack of it, I noticed a connection. When I was enjoying life, money flowed more easily and effortlessly. I started to understand that money is just energy and will flow to us when we are relaxed and at ease. When I worried about money, this actually kept it away.

Here is one of the most important concepts for us to understand about money or lack of it: **We all have programs we are unaware of running about our ability to bring in the money we need. Some of these programs serve us, some of them do not. We will want to look carefully for our negative programs**

DAY 38

so we may start to do the work of clearing them out in order to make room for fresh new abundant programs. Start by asking God and/or your higher self to allow you to see your self-defeating programs. Then, be open to what comes. Simply setting the intention to release these programs will start them clearing. Becoming conscious of an unproductive program takes away much of its power. As we see these programs for what they are, we may start removing them. Many people are running the "there just is never enough money" program.

This may feel very true at the moment but needs to be released in order for a better and more helpful program to be allowed to take root. Take a good look at how your parents handled money.

Were they scared? Did they have enough? Did they spend freely? Now start becoming an outside observer free of attachments or emotional charge, like you would at a stranger's situation. The more we master our ability to see ourselves clearly, the easier it will be to handle these deep fears and let them go. This takes patience and Divine assistance, but we can do it. Give this time. When ready, we want to write out some of the fears we have about money and use our EFT and tools to help clear them out. Focus on clearing unproductive programming and be open to what comes. Fear about money is universal. I will never forget when I read an article about a famous movie actress who was explaining how even though she now made millions of dollars for a TV episode, she was still worried about not having money in the

DAY 38

future. I remember thinking, "Wow, even the 'millionaires' worry, as this is human nature." Let's do this together. Listen hard to the statements you make about money. Are you making comments like, "There is never enough money," "What if I lose my job?" or "When I get old I will run out of money?" It is time to become conscious, pay attention to the statements we make and seek the ones that will serve us best. Sometimes the negative feelings that come up about money, health or love are so intense they actually physically hurt - you can feel them in your gut. But, we have tools to handle them here and now. We no longer have to turn to over-eating, drugs, fighting with others or any other self-destructive behaviors we use to suppress and deny these feelings. Welcome to your power.

Another important understanding to have is that money is an out flowing of Divine energy. One of the most illuminating books I have yet to read on money is *The Abundance Book* by John Randolph Price. This Divine book changed everything for me.

Mr. Price reminds us that money is an effect of our God energy and has no power. **When we worry about money, we give it false power and cut off our supply. All our power and supply comes from our connection to Divine Source, God or however you call your higher self. This Divine Source is flowing through us all the time, thus we are our own supply. Our job is to become conscious of this connection and connect to it.** Be still and let the knowing that God is our never-ending source and supply flow through you. Feel this Divine knowing in your heart

DAY 38

and mind now. Anytime you become fearful about having enough money, health, relationships or happiness say to yourself, **"Everything I need comes to me at the perfect time; I need only relax and have faith."** As you make this decree, feel it deep in your heart and mind and take a deep breath. Feel your abundance and worthiness. Abundance is your birthright; feel this now! This all starts with the conscious connection to your God.

I shall address the belief that desiring money is not "spiritual." Let's be practical: we are living in a time and place where it takes money to live, feel free and secure. We are supposed to have all the vitality, love and money we desire. To say that it is not spiritual to want money is a lot like saying it is wrong to want to eat. Money and spirituality are interrelated. We cannot separate the two because sooner or later the "lessons" that physical money has to offer will call for spirit and Divine guidance. It is then that the Master in all of us can rise to the challenges that money offers. Love and God leads us in how to attract, share and use this money for the highest good of everyone involved. It is my deepest desire to restore this Divine knowing in all of us.

Practice your 44-day plan and infuse your mind with the knowledge that everything you need is flowing to you in Divine time. This creates a safe feeling and gives you peace.

We shall start relaxing now and stop looking to others for our money. This is so empowering because at times we all get attached to the idea that someone -- be it our job, spouse or parent

DAY 38

-- should give us money. Once we release this misconception, it opens up our Divine mind for abundance to flow to us from infinite sources. By looking to a specific person for our safety or money, we actually block so much more. Of course, Divine wisdom will flow our abundance through people and circumstances, but it is not for us to direct from where this money or help will come. We simply allow ourselves to be open to receive now. You are your money and you have all the power. How relaxing and fulfilling is this knowledge? We may not know this overnight, but with practice and use of the 44-day *Activate Your Abundance* plan, we will start to see a rising in our consciousness that lifts and revitalizes our attitudes and life now.

One of the keys to creating more financial prosperity is to take your focus off money and put it on being happy and enjoying the moment. **Money is simply the effect of Divine energy. Money is the physical manifestation of Divine energy -- the source of your supply is God, your Divine Connection.**

Edgar Cayce, the great sleeping prophet, said that all man's physical problems stem from the fear of lack of money. Once we start to make the connection between our natural deep-seated fears about lack and many of the emotional and physical ailments we experience, we can start working on the real source of these problems, clearing out these fears and illusions, making peace with where we are and having faith that we will always have what we need in the moment. The ultimate place to be is free of attachments to our stuff and money.

DAY 38

In Russell Simmons' book *Super Rich,* he explains that attachment to our stuff and money can take all the pleasure out of life and actually create dis-ease. Russell explains that the state of "Super Rich" is knowing that we need nothing because we already have it all. Once again, we are our own supply.

We will clear out these deep-seated fears of lack in order to experience the abundance that is available to every one of us. You will find techniques to clear fear and negative programs. We all have universal fears and negative programs running and we will work on soothing them consistently. As we come to understand our ability to allow everything we need and desire, a deep peace and happiness fills us. We can just let the worry go, relax and enjoy our lives the way we are meant to. Allow Divine knowing to soothe concerns about having enough money and remember that God is our ultimate supply. We shall feel our worthiness and know the magnificence of the God within us in order to line up with all our blessings.

Let your happiness be an indicator of your success. Practice faith and being patient. Get quiet and listen for the Lord on a regular basis. The Lord is the Christ Self or Divine Mind that resides within all of us. Yes, you are abundance personified, and it is time to start seeing yourself this way.

See your money as the giving and receiving of love. I have a good friend whose bracelet I was admiring. I started asking her questions and found out she had created this beautiful bracelet and

DAY 38

sold them in craft shows. All of the sudden, I wanted to buy this from her in order to show how much I appreciated the inspiration and lovely energy she was sharing. I thought, "I have to have this bracelet so I may pay her and give her some love and support." When I asked if it was for sale, her whole face lit up and I could tell she was very flattered and pleased.

We are giving energy and love when we spend money. Appreciate the people you send money to and the ones that send you money. This is a Divine way to enjoy the process of creating more.

Next time you find yourself stressed about having to pay a bill, stop, take a deep breath, and become conscious. First, give thanks that someone believes in your ability to pay. Second, remember that you have an unlimited supply and it is always on its way. My sage grandmother says, "Never worry about anything money can fix." In other words, if we are healthy, this is our true blessing and the rest will take care of itself. As Russell Simmons said, "Money won't make you happy, but happy will make you money." Love it!

Focus on releasing negative, fearful programming and feeling good now. Remember our strength lies in our conscious connection to our God-self. As we relax and line back up with our Divine Mind, we will be given new perfect ideas that bring us joy and fulfillment on all levels. Focus on the Master Creator within; with faith, we know all things are possible.

BLESSING OUR WAY TO VITALITY AND PROSPERITY

"Our prayers should be for blessings in general, for God knows best what is good for us."

---Socrates

A good friend told me the story of how her son, in sales, turned a difficult time around to prosperity. This young man could not even get in to see clients, much less make a sale. This very intelligent lady gave her son a wonderful suggestion. She suggested to her son that he take a moment before going in to make a sales call to bless everyone in the building.

She checked on her son's results a couple of months later and was very pleased with what he had to say. Her son said that just like she had advised, he had taken a few minutes in his car before walking into the sales call to bless everyone in the building. He was amazed at the results. Everyone he called on took the time to see him and make a purchase. He also found himself on the receiving end of Divine ideas. One of his clients did not have time to talk to him because he was on his way home to lunch. My friend's son asked if he could drive this client to his home and pick

DAY 39

him up after his lunch to discuss his product. The client was surprised, but said, "Yes." On the way back from lunch the client was so impressed he placed a big order. This intelligent practice of blessing others can enhance any endeavor we take on.

It is a wonderful practice to say blessings over our food to give it Divine energy before we take it into our bodies. This is the intelligent idea behind prayer before meals.

There have been studies to prove that water responds to our thoughts and actually changes its molecular structure according to the thoughts we send it. Documented pictures show microscopic views of water molecules that have been sent positive thoughts and they are so beautiful. Then, in comparison, pictures of water molecules that have been sent negative thoughts are shown to look distorted. More information on this can be found in the book, *The Hidden Messages of Water* by Masaru Emoto. Since our thoughts are affecting our waters structure, it then follows that the same thing is happening to our food. Before we eat, it is very beneficial to say, "May this food nourish my body and mind," while sending the food some loving energy. We will notice our food digests and even tastes better. I once heard that when a group of camp kids prepared food for people, it tasted extra delicious. When it was investigated, it was found that these kids were not adding anything special to the food but they were very happy and loving while preparing the meals. This resulted in delicious food. Keep this in mind when preparing food. When my family tells me how good my food tastes, I simply tell them that I "added extra love to it" for

DAY 39

them. A revelation flowed to me one day when I was in a horrible mood while eating. All of the sudden I knew this was not in my best interest. So now when I eat, I try to stay conscious and be in a good place mentally. Sometimes I do not remember this until the last bite, but better late than never. I still say, "May this food bless and heal my body," to that last bite. I encourage you to stay conscious and avoid food when you are angry or upset. Herbert Shelton, a famous hygienist, states that even the healthiest foods will turn to poison when we eat them while upset. This is the time to get conscious and abstain from food until the mood passes.

When we bless people, situations, food, and send love, we are guided to a whole new way of conscious thinking that will produce miraculous results. Many masters practice this and now we shall too.

Day 40

COMING FROM OUR PLACE OF POWER

*"We ask ourselves, 'Who am I to be brilliant, gorgeous, talented,
fabulous?' Actually, who are you not to be?"*

---*Marianne Williamson*

Successful people practice something we all can learn
from. They come from their own place of power. This is a place of
confidence and knowing that things always seem to work out for
the best. They believe they deserve the best. Yes, they are the
center of their universe, and my friend, you are the beloved center
of yours.

Your place of power feels like appreciation, love, joy and
contentment. Remember that we are filled with Divine Wisdom
and can do anything. We all have the ability to create anything we
want innate in us. We simply need to come from our place of
power in order to do this. What does this place look and feel like?
It feels like freedom, joy and enthusiasm. It feels like a knowing
that we can do anything we set our minds to. It feels like even
though we do not have all the answers right now, this is alright. We
know they will come at the perfect time -- Divine Timing. It feels
like we are strong and can easily go with the flow. It is an
understanding that even when things do not go our way, everything

DAY 40

is going to work out for the best because we have faith and can focus on what we want, thus shifting things.

A very wise man once advised that if we call any perceived "bad" situation good, then it will have to become so. Anytime something unwanted happens, simply say, "I wonder what blessings will come from this?" This is the place I would love to just "zap" us all to. However, we are the only ones who can do this for ourselves.

It is simply a matter of being dogmatic about focusing on what is working in our lives. As we give our attention to what is working, more things we enjoy will come.

When I hear people speaking of what they do not have and "how hard things are," I want to explain that this is the exact opposite of how we want to focus in order to get our lives back on track. There is a universal law that states that what we put our attention on, we get more of in our life. *It is important that we practice speaking of what we love and enjoy as often as possible.* This will ensure more of what we want coming and encourage us that we are on the right track. Once we understand and start practicing this skill, we will start to feel better and know our power. We are all human, and of course, sometimes this is easier than others. But, we have a goal and we can get there a little each day. It really is about enjoying the journey and not the destination. The destination will take care of itself when we enjoy our lives.

DAY 40

Feeling strong and recognizing our value is a great place to be in order to allow what we want to come. For example, if we say or think, "Wow, things just always seem to work out for me," and "I always get what I want so I shall be patient," this is a much stronger place to come from than saying, "Why is what I want taking so long to come?" They are both saying the same thing in a very different way that will get completely different results. The first statement will serve us much better, as it is charged with faith and knowing.

Here is another comparison. "I am looking better every day," compared to "Why is it taking so long for this exercise program to show results?" The first statement soothes our mind and allows us to be patient in order to line up with feeling and looking our best. Once we understand that everything is working out perfectly, we may relax and come from our place of power.

Bonus

ACCEPTING WHAT IS

"Accepting means you allow yourself to feel whatever it is you are feeling at that moment. It is part of the is-ness of the NOW. You can't argue with what is. Well, you can, but if you do, you will suffer."

---Eckhart Tolle

We have all had situations and people in our lives that we do not like and wish would just go away. Let's discuss the immense benefits of just allowing things to be as they are. When we accept and allow what is, an overwhelming sense of peace will develop as a result. As we surrender to these situations and people just as they are, we may be amazed at what occurs. As we relax and make peace with what is, we release all the resistance that is keeping us stuck. We will also come to understand the many blessings and lessons we are receiving as a result of the "unwanted situation." The quickest way to get unstuck is to get very allowing of all circumstances. We have called them into our lives for a reason. We do not need to understand the reason, only to allow them to "be." This releases any negative attachments that we have, allowing the problem to shift to a better place or disappear.

Once again, getting grounded in the present moment is a wonderful way to help ease into acceptance. We simply remind ourselves that we are safe and can enjoy the moment, knowing we are never alone. God is with us, supporting. If we need to be upset, allow this also. As my sage grandmother says, "This too shall pass," and "Time heals everything." Stay conscious of your connection to your higher power and you will be guided to the perfect solution.

Here is one of my favorite stories about the difference our attitude will make:

A Hasidic Tale
One day a very poor man visited a rabbi. The man complained that he had to live in a tiny one-room house with his wife, six children and mother-in-law. It was so crowded he couldn't stand it any longer; he was losing his mind.
"Do you have any animals?" asked the rabbi.
"Yes, chickens and a goat," the man replied.
"Good," said the rabbi. "Bring the goat into the house to live with you."
The poor man objected, but finally agreed to follow the rabbi's advice. A week later, he came back to the rabbi, even more exasperated. "I brought the goat into my house and now it is worse than before. I can't stand it! What should I do?"
The rabbi instructed, "Go home and bring the chickens into the house to live with you, too." Again the man objected, but finally did as he was told. A week later he came back to the rabbi, dazed and crazed, crying, "It is impossible now in my house, rabbi! Help me!"
The rabbi said, "Go home and take out the goat and the chickens."

Bonus days 37 - 40

The man did as he was told and a few days later came back to the rabbi, smiling and grateful. "Rabbi, my house is now so spacious and peaceful! You are certainly the wisest man who ever lived."

Thanks to Claire Josefine, author of *The Spiritual Art of Being Organized,* for providing this story.

Fulfillment

Each day I focus on the Love that is always flowing through me. I consciously allow this Love to fill me up and guide me throughout my day and my life. I make conscious connection with my God now. I fill my body with deep Divine breaths now. I ponder the idea that I AM part of God and this is my total fulfillment. I take God's Divine Love in with conscious breaths. This Love fills my mind, body and soul. It enhances my life and creates Divine relationships with all the other Godlings around me. I see the love and divinity in everyone and this changes everything. When someone is harsh, I can look at it through new eyes and send the love they are so desperately seeking -- a Divine plea for the love and adoring they are not finding in themselves in the moment. I now see every negative reaction a person has is simply a call for love. I realize we are all human and doing the best we can. I AM easy on myself about this. I answer their call with Divine Love. As I send this love, it comes back to me over and over, fulfilling me on levels I never imagined. I hear God's voice clearer every day as He encourages me to feel this love and put it first. I now accept my Divinity, the fullness of who I truly am. I AM the extension of God energy so I could be nothing if not perfection. I AM beyond blessed by this truth. I see it all so clearly now. I hear God in the birds and breeze, reminding me that He has and always will be with me. I AM Complete.

Day 41

DIVINE RELATIONSHIPS

"The greatest gift that you could ever give to another is your own happiness, for when you are in a state of joy, happiness, or appreciation, you are fully connected to the Stream of pure, positive Source Energy that is truly who you are. And when you are in that state of connection, anything or anyone that you are holding as your object of attention benefits from your attention."

---Esther Hicks

It is natural to have visions of the perfect person coming into our lives and making us utterly blissful. This sounds lovely, but simply will never hold for long periods. None of us are perfect, and looking for completion in another is not fair to ourselves or the other person.

If we are experiencing any problems in our relationships, we must put the attention back where it belongs -- on ourselves! Many of us want to fix everyone else in order to have great relationships. This is a form of avoidance: not wanting to look too closely at our own selves. We are wasting our time trying to change others; the only one we can change is ourselves.

DAY 41

The great news is that as we lift ourselves mentally, we can expect some wonderful results in ourselves, and then as a result, all of our relationships will benefit. It is also very important to remember that we are human and can only do so much. It is in our best interest to set the intention to let Divine Love run through all our relationships in order to get the finest results.

Here is a decree to work with: **"I now ask that Divine Love flow into all my relationships, knowing that everything is in perfect order,"** or **"Divine Love fills me now to enhance all my relationships to a beautiful place."**

Abraham-Hicks reminds us that "it really is about the relationship between you and you." The relationship we are looking to cultivate is between us and our source. We must stop looking to conditions or people to make us feel good. We shall talk lovingly to ourselves now. We will start focusing on things that make us feel good now. As we start realizing that being happy is an inside job and take responsibility for how we feel, we are back in our power. We do not have to depend on one other person; we can cultivate our own bliss and, as a result, reap the untold rewards. Come with me now -- *Take Back Your Power*! Once we are no longer looking to others for our fulfillment, we can relax and enjoy people on a whole new level.

Pay attention to how you talk to yourself. Are you treating yourself with love and respect? If you are having problems with others, start giving yourself all the love and attention you desire.

216

DAY 41

Stop looking to others to make you feel good and start doing it for yourself. This will lift you and all your relationships.

Do not get too attached to the outcomes. When we ask Divine Love to enter our relationships, some of them may fade away to be replaced with more loving and fulfilling ones. Simply allow God to work His miracles and have faith.

Day 42

GIVING WITH LOVE

"For it is in giving that we receive."

---St. Francis of Assisi

I have always been a person who naturally gives things to others. I love the feeling of giving something someone can be enjoying. For me, it is a blessing. I was fascinated when I discovered that some of the wealthiest people in history have been big givers. Moguls like John D. Rockefeller and J. P. Morgan were known for their extreme generosity. At the height of Rockefeller's fortune, he gave about 80% of his funds to charitable organizations. Morgan, on the other hand, was known to have rescued the U.S. economy on two separate occasions. He donated most of his large art collection to the Metropolitan Museum of Art.

People around me question why I give so much away. If they had any idea how much comes back to me, they would completely understand. The most important understanding about giving is to do it with love and a feeling that we are abundant and have plenty to share. There are different ways I give, but one of my favorite stories about giving is to a homeless person because of the blessings it bestowed upon me. My daughters and I were out one snowy, freezing evening. My daughter said "Momma, you need to

DAY 42

turn around. There is a homeless man sitting on a bus bench and it is too cold." We were in the middle of traffic, so I just kept going, thinking this is not really convenient and the only bill I had in my wallet was a hundred. But the more I drove, the more I kept thinking I need to do something for this guy. So I turned around and found him. He was shivering and hidden beneath his jacket. I walked up and shook his hand. I handed him the money and he looked at me a little shocked and a little like a kid on Christmas.

He said, "Why did you do that?" I said, "I don't know; I just want to." The real power was in the unspoken words we exchanged. We both felt "we are connected" and smiled at each other. It was a moving experience I will never forget and the man could never have received as much as he gave me that evening. When I got back in the car my girls and I were giddy. We felt like we had made a little difference, like we were helping in our little corner of the universe.

The Divine Catherine Ponder explains that giving creates a vortex for all that is good to come to us. Giving comes from our place of power. We are essentially saying, "I am so abundant that I can give freely." The universe responds to this by bringing more of what is wanted to us. It is important to give with love in our heart and from an inspired place; this will come back to us over and over.

Florence Shinn, a great prosperity author, explains that we cannot ask for things and give nothing in return; this defies law. As

DAY 42

we give with love in our hearts, we bring many desired things to us. She tells the story of a young mother who did not have the funds to give her children a Christmas holiday or dinner. It was explained to the young woman that she needed to say a prayer for what she needed and then give something in return. She was told to set her table and expect a wonderful Christmas feast. The young mother was perplexed, as she felt she had nothing to give. Shinn told her that everyone has something to give and to pray on it. After quiet contemplation, the young woman realized she wanted to take her sick neighbor some flowers she had in her yard. The young woman cut her flowers and took them to her neighbor. Her neighbor was thrilled to get the flowers and attention. Then she and her children set a lovely table, which got them all excited and happy. Later that day, the young mother received an unexpected payment on a long forgotten debt that she never expected to see again. This money bought the women and her children a lovely dinner and holiday. Giving in faith and love allows for miracles.

Day 43

GIVE LOVE WITH NO EXPECTATIONS

*"Your task is not to seek for love,
but merely to seek and find all of the barriers within yourself
that you have built against it."*

---A Course in Miracles

When we give love, we usually expect it to come back from the exact person we gave it to. Let's just release this "old school" thinking right now for our benefit. Here is how it works. When we give love, it comes back to us many times over from many and varied sources. If we are busy expecting this love from a certain person, we are going to miss all the good stuff coming to us. Once we understand this law, we can give love, know it is coming back to us, and just sit back and enjoy all the "happy surprises" coming our way.

When we give love, we want to stay open for God to return it. Then, we may become an open vessel that will be filled with love. For example, if someone is angry and upset, send them love and do not expect anything in return. You will be doing both of you a Divine favor. This love will be sent back to you many times. The idea is to become unattached to who brings you this love.

DAY 43

We are all family, and many times our "true family" is not related to us. Once we become open to love and stop being picky about the "face" it comes with, this allows all sorts of love from family and friends. Deep self-love is the perfect way to enhance any relationship. Here is a visualization that will bring more love and peace into our relationships from the *Stress Free Meditation CD* by Deepak Chopra:

*Sit with your eyes closed; feet on the ground. You may play soft relaxing music if you desire. Visualize a person you want to get along better with. See them smiling at you and look deep into their eyes. Hold this picture for a few minutes. Mentally communicate with them how much you love them for another few minutes. Now say to them, **"I am worthy, I love and find myself perfect just as I am."** Any relationship is enhanced by our own deep self love. Now hold this thought while making eye contact with them in your mind's eye. See yourself giving them a hug or a form of affection that feels good to you. Feel great love between the two of you for a few minutes. Laugh and play with this person in your mind. Expect miracles. When we are having difficulties with someone we love or want to love, we can do this and get miraculous results. This is the power of love visualization.*

Day 44

EVERYTHING YOU WANT WAITS

"Follow your bliss and the universe will open doors where there were only walls."

---Joseph Campbell

I can confidently remind you that everything you want is patiently waiting for you – *NO ONE* else has access to it! There is no competition for resources. Once we understand this, we can relax into our Divine inheritance. Abraham-Hicks reminds us that everything we want is already created and just waiting for us to line up with it. Sounds iffy, I know. Here is how it works and where our faith will be very important.

There is a part of us that is always connected to God or the Divine. This part of us knows everything we want and how to get it better than our human mind can imagine. Everything we want is already created with our Divine energy and simply waiting for us to line up with it. We created it with God, a co-creation. Our work is done. Now, all we need to do is relax and start enjoying our blessings. This allows us to line up with what our Divine energy has created. As we get happy and start appreciating what we have, we shall see evidence that we are on the right track. This is why

DAY 44

appreciation is such a powerful tool. Appreciation quiets the ego and allows our God mind to flow freely.

Our abundance comes to us in our own unique time and style. There is never any need to compete with another. Bless others for their good fortune and know ours is coming. It is always productive to be happy for what others have. This serves us on many levels. There is an abundance of all things wanted and more than enough for everyone. It is a common human fear that "there is just not enough for everyone." The tapping technique discussed in this book is perfect for helping us to release fear. It is so important to release fear so it does not attract unwanted situations and people to us. It is one of those old computer programs we must delete in order to thrive. You may use your EFT tapping or any of the other processes for removing negative emotions and programs here in your book with great success.

I love the line from the book *Illusions* by Richard Bach, "The Is has imagined it better than you could." This line eloquently reminds us that the "Is," which is God energy, knows how to bring about the perfect circumstances at the perfect time, better than our human mind can ever imagine. So our job is simply to relax, have faith and follow our guidance. While writing this book, I was listening to an Abraham-Hicks CD and I smiled as I heard Jerry Hicks ask Abraham a question relating to this. Hicks stated that he loved this same line from the book *Illusions*. Abraham explained the meaning of the line in this way: that throughout our lives we have desired things. We have been putting all these desires out

Day 44

there and do not even remember many of them, some of them even from when we were babies. They explained that "source energy" knows every one of the desires we have ever had and is lovingly holding them for us and simply waiting for us to allow them to manifest. We all have this vast array of dreams just waiting for us to allow them.

FAITH

"Faith ... is being sure of what you hope for and certain of what you do not see."

---Hebrews 11:1(NIV)

Our knowing that everything is working out for the best can be one of our strongest assets. It has been said that faith can move mountains, so we will want to cultivate ours now. As we remember that great things are possible, we magnetize them to ourselves. Creating more of what we want is about having faith that when we put our best out there, it is always coming back to us, and it is. This is law.

One of the best ways we can build faith is to ask for help and just be open to it and in positive expectation. Recently, I was feeling quite low. I felt like there was really no need for another "motivational" book in the world. I was questioning why I was writing another. During a particularly rough day where I was clearing a lot of negative energy, I said, "Please, someone just give me a sign that what I am doing is on the right path for me, while helping others." The next day a lovely woman called to tell me that my first book, *How Green Smoothies Saved My Life,* had really helped her. She said that she was feeling very bad and felt God led her right to that book. She proceeded to tell me how much better she was doing as a result of using some of the ideas in that book. I

Bonus days 41 - 44

was in awe and had tears in my eyes as this wonderful woman spoke because I knew she was my sign. The bliss I felt at that moment was indescribable because I knew God was talking to me through this sweet woman. When we allow these signs and blessings to come to us, there is an overwhelming feeling that "Yes! God is listening and answering us all the time." Asking for help and allowing it will cultivate wonderful faith and remind us that we are never alone.

We must ask, though, as God and the angels practice free will and will never impose help. It must be sought by us.

Having faith is understanding that when we decide to let go and let God, we can relax and let the Divine Energy that has created worlds flow though our life. We do not need to get in and micromanage the situation. This message has been given to us over and over. Now, it is time to listen and let this Divine knowing fill our body, mind and spirit with the belief that when we align with our higher selves - our God - all things are possible. **As we set the intention to "be still and know God," the perfect message does come at the perfect time.** This is where our meditation can help to be still and hear that Divine Wisdom from within. This love is flowing to us constantly; all we have to do is become conscious and allow it. **Faith will clear this Divine channel and make way for amazing blessings.**

Any time we are going through challenges, it is more important than ever to get centered and remember our divinity. Just

Bonus days 41 - 44

take one minute at a time and fill it with the knowing that everything will be alright no matter what happens.

I went through a really hard time physically and was faced with a medical procedure I did not want. I was very upset and quite out of alignment. I cried to a very wise friend that I just did not know what to do and was very scared. She intelligently explained to me that things would be alright no matter what. She said it with such conviction and knowing that I felt it was true. I remember thinking, "Yes, I know she is right. I am going to be alright." It did not happen overnight, but I came to the understanding that I would be fine either way and was guided to do what was best for me in the situation.

When we have a "problem," our best course of action is to calm down, have faith and get clear in order to allow all the Divine guidance that is available to flow through and to us. If we try to take action from a fearful place, we are probably not going to like the results.

Close your eyes right now, take a deep breath and just feel how truly safe you are. Let the knowing that all is well fill your heart and mind. A soothing affirmation to say is: **"Everything is fine right now; I can relax and just be."** Guess what? My wise friend was correct! Once I got centered, everything worked out so much better than I could have ever imagined. I also received many blessings in the way of a more open mind, understanding of others and renewed zest for life as a result of having gone through this unwanted situation. Our greatest challenges are blessings in

Bonus days 41 - 44

disguise. Richard Bach states this perfectly in his wonderful book, *Illusions*: **"There is no such thing as a problem without a gift for you in its hands. You seek problems because you need their gifts."**

As we have faith that everything will work out for the best in the end, we allow great things to come to us. Hope and faith bring the perfect solutions.

Once at 2:00 in the morning, our daughter called from a friend's house to say she was not feeling well and wanted to come home. There was a bad storm and it was dark, but my husband bravely got up to go get her. When he returned with her safe, I thanked him. He said, "When she calls, we will come." These words resonated with me so strongly. I thought that is how God is - *if we call, He will come.*

We do not need to know all the answers now; things do unfold at the perfect time for the best results possible. Remember that it is not what happens to us, but how we respond to it. We can respond with faith and hope to allow miracles.

Author's Note

"Our birth is but a sleep and a forgetting: the soul that rises with us, our life's star, hath had elsewhere its setting, and cometh from afar. Not in entire forgetfulness, and not in utter nakedness, but trailing clouds of glory do we come from God, who is our home."

---William Wordsworth

In Russel Simmons' book *Super Rich*, which I consider "required reading," he tells an inspiring story from the sacred text the Bhagavad Gita. This is one of the most loved Hindu books and is filled with the wisdom of the ages. I have yet to study this book that has inspired millions, so I was thrilled to have Simmons interpret it for us. He tells the story of Lord Krishna and a human. The human says to Lord Krishna, who is a God, "Show me who you are. I must see your God self." Lord Krishna explains to the human that he is not advanced enough to look at the real Lord Krishna. The man begs and Lord Krishna agrees to show his God self. The Lord Krishna starts turning into a sweet young baby, then an old dying man, then a beautiful sunset, then a terrible storm, then a beautiful woman, then a man killing another. The human starts becoming overwhelmed with all the images flashing before him and begs Lord Krishna to stop. Lord Krishna stops. The man gets the beautiful message that everything is God, all of it, the good and the bad. This story moved me and sank in to create more understanding and peace.

One day I was at the hospital visiting a friend. It was a rainy, dreary day. I was thinking, "I wish it were sunny." I have never been a fan of the rain. All of the sudden it became so clear how perfect this day was. I realized the beauty in this rainy day. It was like I finally understood that it was just as lovely as the sunniest day. Then I stared at my "sick" beloved friend and realized he was perfect just like he was. I just sat there in awe enjoying the moment. I told my brilliant daughter this story and she said, "You have to put this in the book." So here it is, the reminder, **it is all God**. The good and bad is God. We do not have to understand it all, but we can accept and allow the things we do not like or understand with a little more peace in order to experience Divine states.

As I write this book, I feel it will never be complete. This is because, as you know, we are always learning and finding more on subjects we love. So please remember this is just a starting place and you will add many more ideas and concepts. It always tickles me how I will read over something I have written when I am having a hard day and it will lift and bring me back. I will think, "Who wrote this?" Well as you know, I just allowed the Divine energy to flow as I wrote. So I do not take any credit, I only feel honored to be a part of something I love and enjoyed every minute of. I do not have all the answers and I never like to imply I do.

I wrote this book because I have a burning desire to help people with the Divine knowledge I have acquired through years of study, but I understand that there are times when people just do not want to hear this. I mean, if we are having a really bad day or experience, we do not want to hear, "You create your own reality." When someone is really ready, they can pick up this or any other motivational book and get what they need. God is always talking to us; *"if you call, he will come."*

Blessings to you and yours, Kim Caldwell

Kim Caldwell lives in Memphis Tennessee with her husband Jimmy and beautiful daughters Clair and Rachel. She graduated from the University of Memphis and has studied how our thoughts and nutrition affect our lives for two decades. Check out the *Activate Your Abundance* audios and her other book *How Green Smoothies Saved My Life* at www.togetherpublishing.com.

CONCLUSION

"To thine own self be true, and it must follow, as the night the day, thou canst not then be false to any man."

---William Shakespeare

We have covered a lot of Divine ground here and I am honored that you took the time to read this. Did I write this? No, but I am sure by now you know where this information flowed from. As a teenager, it was a personal dream of mine to be a cheerleader. It was not in the cards for me then, but now I consider myself a cheerleader and I am cheering you on all the way. See, dreams do come true.

It is my greatest desire that you take the information that is best for you and create blessings and abundance on all levels in your life. I also remind you to use only the information that feels good for you. Keep the best and leave the rest.

We have started an amazing process of lifting our consciousness and, when practiced consistently, this serves every area of our life. You may just want to sit with the knowing or do the 44-day program again. You know what is best for you. When, however, you are having a difficult day, feel free to get out the program and pick a meditation that lifts you. Practice makes perfect.

Remember, we are all doing the best we can in every moment. Never look to anyone else for the answers, as all the wisdom you need is waiting deep within you. Be easy about all this and enjoy the process -- there is no wrong way to do it. You Are Perfect! You Are Divine! I look forward to hearing your success stories at www.togetherpublishing.com.

Thank You

Thank you to my beautiful husband Jimmy for loving and supporting me every day.

Thank you to my beautiful daughter Clair for teaching me about energy alignment and sharing her brilliance.

Thank you to my beautiful daughter Rachel for being an energizer bunny and showing us all how it is done.

Thank you to my Aunt Rita for her love and invaluable support and editing skills.

Thank you to my mom Jeri for setting a good example of a strong intelligent woman and being the glue that keeps us together.

Thank you to my Me Me who always has a wonderful attitude and shares it with everyone.

Thank you to my beautiful sister Blair who lives this book more than most and sets an outstanding example, and Lane for keeping Blair in line.

Thank you to Jessica for her sweetness and wisdom.

Thank you to Reed for being our man in a family of women.

Thank you to my father for his devotion to his family.

Thank you to my delightful sister n law Sandy who makes me laugh all the time and needs to put out her own book.

Thank you to Michael, Cameron and Lincoln for bringing the fun.

Thank you to my amazing neighbors who make our lives better for just being.

Thank you to Jamey for our walks and talks.

Thank you to Pam for her strong guidance and support.

Thank you to Annie for her never-ending sweetness and love.

Thank you to Cindy for her continued support with editing.

Thank you to Cheiro for charging the book with Love and Switchwords to lift us.

Thank you to Amina McIntyre for her amazing contributions to this book.

Thank you to CJ for her friendship and amazing contribution to the book.

Thank you to Milton Craft for his Divine Timing.

Thank you to the amazing authors I have been blessed to study and share here.

Testimonials

What others are saying about

How Green Smoothies Saved My Life also

by Kim Caldwell

"I am writing to let you know that since discovering your book and embarking on a daily 'Green Smoothie' I am feeling the enormous benefits. I am a fitness coach and have been recommending your book to all my clients, if you would like to have a look at my website www.angiedowds.com you can see the kind of work I do, I am not sure if you are familiar with the TV show 'Biggest Loser' but I am the female trainer on the UK version and have had incredible results over the last 3 shows and I am about to start filming the next season in September."

Kind Regards Angie

"Kim, one day I walked into Whole Foods and was so sick. That day God just led me straight to you. I started telling you how sick I was and you offered to give me the book *How Green Smoothies Save My Life* to help. I began to follow the instructions in the book and I noticed how much strength and energy I had as opposed to before when I was very weak. Since then my health has improved. I finally got to the section "choose your words wisely"

Testimonials

and I was blown away because I do believe in being positive but when you're sick you can't rise above it and this helped. I also like the part in the book about placing your hand over where you feel sick and sending love to your body. I love this book. I would suggest it to anyone."

Thank you Cora Pulley

"Just received Kim's book yesterday...fabulous! Almost finished Thank you so much! She is sensitive, practical, inspirational, and very motivating...she hands you the spiritual, mental & physical tools on a platter!"

xoxo Sylvia

"My wife has taken on a look like when she was younger. Certain lines in her face have melted away. It has been only a couple of weeks now on green smoothies. You know how men develop what they call "love handles"? Well mine have almost completely gone away. Me and my wife have not looked this good for a number of years. Thank you so much for your book *How Green Smoothies Saved My Life*.

We read it out loud and are, at this moment drinking Green Smoothies as I write this. Your book, in my opinion, is must reading for all those who choose to develop a healthy respect and love for their body, mind, and spirit.

Testimonials

Kim, I believe that *How Green Smoothies Saved My Life* is one of the most essential books to have and to study. This book can actually not only give good living tips, but save millions and millions of people from needless suffering around the world. Billions of people!"

Thanks again, Cheiro

"I just wanted to let you know that I got the book yesterday. I read it in one shot and I just want to thank you so much! When I was 12-14 I lost 6 very close family members, in that time period, and dealing with the grief, I figured out that I could be happy and fulfilled on my own, regardless of the emotions of those around me. As I got a little older, and got more stress and responsibility in my life I'd started to forget all of that, and almost stopped believing in it. I just wanted to say thank you for reminding me, as well as enriching the concept so much further. I already feel so much more excited about day to day life. I'll be recommending your book to everyone I know and keeping mine by my bed to read when I need another reminder :)"

Many thanks, Jocelyn

"Kim's book is a true blessing in anyone's life. Every part of it is filled with nuggets of information. Just turning the pages get me lifted! I particularly love the switch words section and the processes of sending love to all, the allowance of forgiveness. I know that whenever I am a bit off I can turn to the pages for a huge lift. What is most beautiful about this book is that Kim talks of these tools that anyone of us can incorporate in our lives. We can

Testimonials

really transform our lives with these essential ideas and none of these take a great deal of our time because they are so simple! Being with the book is like having my best friend who is across the oceans, right there beside me. I have the book kept right beside my bed along with Louise Hay and Abraham Hicks books. I know whenever I am in need for a feeling of body lift; I can get awesome green smoothie ideas. Every page is a power house of some of the most amazing tools that we can tap into, in the universe."

Thanks infinitely! Aishwarya (India)

"Kim your book has helped me tremendously. Smoothies are great for my health. Thanks to you, I've stopped artificial sweeteners and corn syrup. Choosing words wisely and using "switchwords" have helped my mental well-being. I've lost 2 pounds. Kim you are definitely making a positive difference in my life. I thank God for you. "Sincerely, Jestine.

"These pages are filled with useful practical knowledge that when put to use will radically change the way you live! Find your well being starting with uplifting thinking and green smoothies as Kim guides you on a path to happiness."

Jessica Levesque- Author of *Embracing Birth: A Collection of Inspiring Birth Stories*

CPSIA information can be obtained at www.ICGtesting.com
Printed in the USA
LVOW041330260912

300419LV00001B/41/P